A Born L

My Rugby League life

Harry Pinner

London League Publications Ltd

A Born Leader
My Rugby League life
Harry Pinner

© Harry Pinner. Foreword © Eamonn McManus. Introduction © Billy Benyon. The moral right of Harry Pinner to be identified as the author has been asserted.
Cover design © Stephen McCarthy.
Cover photos: Front: Playing for Great Britain against New Zealand in 1985 (Courtesy *Rugby League Journal*). Back: In action for St Helens (Andrew Cudbertson)

All photographs are as credited to the photographer or provider of the photo. No copyright has been intentionally breached; please contact London League Publications Ltd if you believe there has been a breach of copyright.

A CIP catalogue record for this book is available from the British Library.

First published in Great Britain in April 2016 by London League Publications Ltd, PO Box 65784, London NW2 9NS

ISBN: 978-1-909885-12-7

Cover design by Stephen McCarthy Graphic Design, 46, Clarence Road, London N15 5BB

Editing and layout by Peter Lush

Printed and bound in Great Britain by Charlesworth Press, Wakefield

This book is dedicated to my wife, Anne and our lovely family. A special mention must also go to my rugby league mentor and good friend George Nicholls.

Foreword

Just as Paul Wellens is the 'Mr St Helens' of this generation, Harry Pinner is that of my generation.

He had it all, and he gave it all to the Saints. By our club's historic standards, his 12 seasons at the club were somewhat light in silverware, but Harry must go down as one of our all-time great players. At times he almost singlehandedly carried the team. His ability was only matched by his bravery and he represented his country as well as his club with equal pride and dedication.

From deepest, darkest Parr he went to the fabled Derbyshire Hill School. There could have been no better preparation for the war zone of professional rugby league in the 1970s and 1980s in which he excelled.

Everyone knows Harry as one of the great players and great leaders of our great club. I know him better as a great friend. He is as modest as he is generous in spirit. He only speaks well of everyone and everything, and it's one of my greatest privileges as Chairman of St Helens to get to know him as a friend as well as a great past Saint.

I'm sure his book will be as illuminating as it will be interesting.

The greatest Saint of his time and forever the gentleman. Proud to know you Harry.

Eamonn McManus
Chairman
St Helens RFC

Introduction: The rubber stamp of greatness

I first met Harry when he arrived at Knowsley Road as a youngster in the early 1970s and he made an immediate impression on me with his sheer dedication. He wanted to be successful and from being one of the younger players coming through from the 'A' Team – I was in the later stages of my career – it was obvious that he was going to be a great player. Later, of course, when I took over as coach at Saints, Harry was the natural choice as captain. Everyone looked up to him and he was a valued ally as we looked towards regaining Saints' place in the rugby league elite. He had, by this time, matured into a superb leader. He had a phenomenal work rate and would always demand extra from the players and certainly led by example. It is this quality in particular that earned him the respect of his team-mates at Knowsley Road.

English loose forwards have been renowned for their ball-handling ability more than ever and Harry Pinner is up there with the very best of them: Johnny Whiteley, Rocky Turner, Bill Major, Steve 'Knocker' Norton and the like. Growing up in St. Helens in the 1950s and watching the Saints, however, the number 13 jersey meant only one player: Vince Karalius. He was rough, tough and dominated the scrum-base, frightening opposing scrum-halves to death, especially if they even thought about going round the blind-side. He was also a creative player, with huge hands like spades to take the ball up to the opposition ready for the off-loaded pass. He also helped along the career of his scrum-half, Alex Murphy and they went on to play test match rugby together in Australia and New Zealand. Vince was the loose forward that all future number 13s at St Helens had to measure up to.

There was one game in particular that I remember that show-cased Harry's undoubted brilliance. It was against Hull FC at Knowsley Road, on 22 March 1985. It was a game we needed to win, as we were chasing the First Division title with our biggest rivals Hull KR ahead of us. So we needed the points to keep in contention. We led 17–12 at half-time and then completely blitzed them in the second half to win 47–18. Overall we scored nine tries and they were all belters. The game was televised as part of *RL Action*, on Granada Television. There would be highlights of the first 40, then the whole of the second half. The programme was hosted by Elton Welsby, who was a real Saints fan. The commentator was Keith Macklin, with Vince Karalius doing the summarising.

Saints' brand of fast, open football made for perfect viewing. Vinty certainly knew what he was talking about when it came to anyone with the number 13 on his back and was fulsome in his praise for Harry and his almost-perfect attacking performance. This was truly the rubber stamp of greatness, from one of the game's all-time greats, which spoke volumes for me about Harry's status in the game at the time.

I certainly agreed with everything Vinty said. It was a real masterclass from Harry, who displayed all his marvellous skills and was the catalyst for one of the most exciting team performances I have ever witnessed as a Coach. The players of the mid-1980s had a license to go out and do what they were best at. I believe that it is important not to stifle talent at any level and to let players express themselves at the expense of regimentation, which seems to dominate the modern game. At the end of the day they were there to entertain the crowd and produced a superb spectacle. Everything Harry did that evening came off. Harry knew exactly what needed to be done. He was a great tactician. He was brilliant with the ball in his hands and he had an excellent kicking game. Although he was on the small side, he would work hard in defence and set the standard for others to follow. Against Hull he was the perfect decision-maker. He knew when to pass and when to run. Like all the best players, he had the vision to anticipate how things would develop several passes in advance.

It was always seen as a privilege to play for a club like the Saints and local lads like Harry, in particular, carried a great sense of pride with them when they went out onto the pitch and they wanted to please the crowd. It was second nature to them. It was a different competition then, with players being largely part-time, but they still had to put the time in and preparation was taken seriously. For a Sunday game, we would have a 'loosener' on a Monday; train on Tuesdays and Thursdays and come in for a final session on a Saturday morning, but there was an emphasis on speed and ball work. During the Hull game, apart from Harry's promptings, the players supported each other superbly and the forwards were never afraid to release the ball. It was fabulous stuff.

Although we just failed to secure the league title – Hull KR won in the end by three points – the game provided a brilliant snapshot of what the Saints should always be about – great entertainers. When I was a player in the 1960s, our coach, Joe Coan, emphasised the need to be physically fit to win matches and the Saints of 1985 certainly were, but they also had pace in abundance. This went right through the team, from winger Barry Ledger, inside back Mal Meninga, scrum-half Neil Holding, back-rower Andy Platt, all co-ordinated by Harry at loose forward. They would cause havoc and could score tries from anywhere and, in Sean Day, had a guy who kicked a high percentage of his goals. All-in-all a recipe for success and, at the end of the 1984–85 season, we had two trophies on the sideboard – the Lancashire Cup and Premiership Trophy – not a bad haul. We looked to improve still further with the young side we had. Unfortunately, things did not quite develop as Harry and I would have liked, but one thing I will always remember is how loyal he was to me as a coach. That loyalty and respect was mutual, believe me.

Billy Benyon

Acknowledgements

Although I had a memorable career in rugby league, it never really occurred to me to put down my memories in book form. Over the past few years, a part of me has been saying 'why not' and although some of the events may not be crystal clear over time, I think that the story is interesting and shows what happened at Saints during rare years of decline, when the team was gradually built up again to become capable of challenging for major honours. In fact, the whole book revolves around highs and lows at both club and international level, but I wouldn't have missed playing rugby for the world.

As for making this happen, I would like to thank first and foremost my wife, Anne and our lovely family, who encouraged me to 'have a go'. I also valued in particular the informal chats with Saints' historian Alex Service, over many cups of coffee, and Geoff Cropper, who helped me to remember different events in my career. It is always difficult for a player to recall certain things, but the fans always seem to remember them. They never miss a trick.

The quotes at the start of each chapter are mostly taken from my Testimonial Brochure, from 1985. Some of the members of my former Testimonial Committee are no longer with us, but even so, they did such a great job on my behalf all those years ago and I will never forget them. I also must mention George Nicholls, once again, for his help and encouragement when I first came to St Helens.

I would like to thank Saints' Chairman Eamonn McManus for his help and encouragement and for the brilliant Foreword. The club now enjoys life at a new stadium with great training facilities and has come a long way from the 1980s. Geoff Pimblett and Steve Leonard also help to keep me in touch with events at the club and it is much appreciated. Thanks also to Billy Benyon for his Introduction and Adrian Lawrenson for proof reading

Photographs have been provided by Alex Service, Brian Peers – Saints' photographer of the 1980s in all weathers, Harry Edgar from *Rugby League Journal*, Bill Appleton, Andrew Cudbertson, Curtis Johnstone and Richard, who provided some excellent family pictures.

Special thanks to Peter Lush and Dave Farrar at London League Publications Ltd for giving me the chance to recall my time in rugby league.

Harry Pinner

London League Publications Ltd would like to thank Alex Service for his assistance to Harry on the book, Steve McCarthy for designing the cover and the staff at Charlesworth Press for printing the book.

Contents

Coach and captain: Billy Benyon and Harry Pinner meet the dignitaries before the 1984 Lancashire Cup Final at Central Park, Wigan. It was Harry Pinner's first trophy as a Saint and Billy was full of praise for his team that day: "They were magnificent. They overwhelmed Wigan with brilliant first-half football and defended bravely after the break. I felt moved at the final hooter. The first players I saw were Harry Pinner and Peter Gorley, and I saw how much winning the cup meant to them."

1. Excelling at sport!

"No-one has ever worn that number 13 for St Helens with greater pride or distinction than Harry Pinner."
Vince Karalius

Rugby in my DNA

For as long as I can ever remember, sport has played such a big part in my life. I remember when I was aged 15 watching my local team, St Helens, take on mighty Leeds in the Challenge Cup at Wembley in 1972. Saints won a really thrilling game and I dreamed about playing there one day – for St Helens of course! If you are born in the town and you like rugby league, that's what every schoolboy wants to do, and I was no exception. My father took me to watch my first Saints' game when I was six and I decided more or less straightaway that my favourite player wore the number 13 jersey – Duggie Laughton, who was a Widnes lad, but he played for my favourite team! He was a magical player; so much play revolved around him and he always seemed to have so much time and space to work in. He was a natural star and knew when to make a break or to find support. Not only did I want to play like him, but little did I realise that Duggie would become a good friend and a great off-field influence especially at the latter end of my own rugby league career.

What else could I do in sport? Rugby league was in my DNA. But there was another influence on my mother's side. Her brother was Ike Fishwick a tough-as-teak hooker who played with distinction for Saints, Warrington, Liverpool City and Blackpool Borough during his career. I was also very close to his brother, Bill, who was a bit of a utility player at Saints during and after the War.

Uncle Ike was a real character and, quite naturally, I looked up to him and he also took a strong interest in my sporting career as well. Ike certainly liked to get stuck in during his playing days and was sent off no less than seven times during his career. I have a newspaper article about him at home and part of it says: "I think the tough guy tag was a bit undeserved. I never started trouble but I was ready to mix it. I got more hidings than I gave though. There were one or two lads I always used to mix it with, like Dave Cotton at Warrington and Joe Egan and Ken Gee at Wigan, but that is just part of the game. I was sent off a few times, but I think the refs had the wrong idea about me. You could say I was victimised." That sounds very much like the Uncle Ike I knew. Ike was a stalwart of the Saints team that was re-built after the war ended and he faced little competition for the number nine jersey until the signing of Welshman Reg Blakemore in 1947–48. Ike played his last match for the

1

Saints on 6 November 1948 against Salford and joined Warrington. He shared a benefit at Knowsley Road with centre Jim Stott, who had joined the club at the same time before the Second World War. He was also a bit of a mould-breaker, a tough rugby league hooker, who went on to lift the Challenge Cup with Warrington, whose hobby, believe it or not, was ballroom dancing.

Ike moved to Norfolk where his wife, my auntie Win, was from. He worked as a foreman with a fertiliser firm in Great Yarmouth. By the early 1970s they became involved in the holiday chalet business. He kept quite fit after he finished playing and was only a few pounds above his playing weight – 13 and a half stones – but he always used to say that it was the dancing that kept him in trim. To some it could have been perceived as being 'sissy', but no-one would have said that to him! He passed away in his early fifties and I still miss him to this day.

Ike's brother, my uncle Bill, played his first game for Saints against their deadly rivals, St Helens Recs at Knowsley Road on Boxing Day 1938. He played on the right wing and kicked a goal, but despite his efforts the visitors came away with a 5–4 win. A Welshman called Stan Powell was his centre. Bill played against the visiting New Zealander tourists, who only played two matches before they had to go back home, when War was declared. He was in the second row this time, but could not prevent the Kiwis from coming away from Knowsley Road with a 19–3 victory. Bill and Ike played together for the Saints during part of the war years.

Bill went on to serve in the Parachute Regiment and returned to Knowsley Road, playing the last of his 76 matches for the club at loose forward against Hull KR at Craven Park on 17 January 1948. He scored a try, but the Saints went down 17–10. Bill, who was very much a utility player, later went to Barrow for a spell. He remained a bachelor throughout his life. A lovely man, he worked for St Helens Council for more than 30 years in the Highways Department, but suffered a stroke in the late 1970s. I remember taking him to some of the earliest get-togethers of the Saints' Past Players Association, where he used to have a good chat with some of his old team-mates. Sadly, he passed away in a Parr nursing home early in 1984.

So these family links are the reasons why I was so interested in sport more or less from the off. Both my parents were from St Helens, the Pocket Nook/Merton Bank area. In fact, when I was born in 1956, we lived in Merton Bank Road, opposite Merton Bank School. The Head teacher was the great Saints' chairman Harry Cook for a spell. My dad, Harry, was originally in the Merchant Navy. He later worked on the railways as a Guard for most of his life, although he was later transferred to what was known as the 'Powerbox' at Warrington, which involved signalling, after he became ill. He also kennelled for people who went on holidays. Perhaps this is where I began my own desire to keep [and later breed] dogs, especially bulldogs. Dad married Connie [Constance] when they were both in their late20s and their first child, my elder sister Patricia, preceded me by four years.

Mum was a real grafter and worked at a butcher's shop called Dewhirst's in Fingerpost for a spell and later at BICC Burndy, at Sutton. My parents did their best to provide for us and we always had an annual holiday together. We used to go to places like Skegness and sometimes to Cornwall, although my favourite place was probably Blackpool – there was everything there for kids and we used to love going on the fair. It is true to say that it was good to have an elder sister, because in the early days she would always look after me and keep me out of potential trouble. I still did manage to get in bother. I remember I got a rugby ball for my birthday and I used to do place-kicks on the grass verges next to the road. The trouble was, I used to do them in front of Mrs Lunt's house, digging in with my heel to make a hole for the ball before I kicked it. She always used to go mad and frequently chased me away!

A sports mad youngster

We later moved to Waring Avenue, in Parr. My first schooling was at Derbyshire Hill Junior and Infant School and one of the teachers there, Roy Grice, used to run much of the sport. His brother, Alan, used to play rugby league for Salford. He was a football man, although that didn't bother me in the slightest. I just loved sport – any sport. It was the be-all and end-all of my existence. My school reports were predictably similar, along the lines of "Harry must concentrate more. He always has his mind on sport etc etc". It was easily my favourite lesson, although I didn't actually dislike what was on offer during the rest of the time at school. I loved to play football in the winter and cricket in the summer. I seemed to remember I had a liking for Manchester City from an early age, with the likes of Alan Oakes, Tommy Booth and Glyn Pardoe, but I never went to the games. Mind you...they are the first result I look for these days. Apart from dreaming of winning cups with the Sky Blues, the inter-school rivalry was fierce and matches against local rivals like Parr Flats were eagerly anticipated.

I used to play sport all the time with my mates and we used to climb over the fence and play on the school field whenever we could. Some of the lads who I used to play football with there were four or five years older than me and I suppose I learned to take knocks. It wasn't all football, though. My dad was a keen fisherman and I used to go with him when he went to places like Carr Mill Dam, where we would fish for roach and perch and also the famous 'Hotties' near the town centre, where the water was warm after it had been used to cool the glass-making tanks at Pilkingtons. There were tropical fish in there too. Fishing

3

was a great way for father and son to bond together and when I was aged about 14 I used to go with my dad to the River Dee at Sutton Green. One day, he caught this huge 18 pound salmon. It's a day that sticks out in my memory as much as any other occasion in my life, especially when I helped to land this monster fish. It was really strong and powerful.

Needless to say I failed my 11 Plus exam that would have meant a grammar school education and began at Parr Central School. This had a fine reputation for sport and two Saints' players of the 1950s, Frank Carlton and John 'Todder' Dickinson were former pupils. My first day was memorable – for the wrong reasons! I didn't attend for the first couple of days – I think we were coming back from our holidays – and it was Wednesday when I made my first appearance.

The first lesson was sport and we got changed in what was almost like a cellar. This lad came over to me and said: "Are you Pinner, the cock of Derbyshire Hill? We'll see who the boss is now"! It was basically a challenge in the time-honoured way, but I was not in the least bit interested in what this guy was on about. In the end, I threw one of my rugby boots at him. The long metal studs actually caused a cut on his head. I think I got sent home for that – on my first day.

But I suppose neither of us got round to deciding who was the 'Cock of First Year' and we just used to ignore each other after that. Let me say straight away that I was never guilty of bullying. But I would sort a bully out if I had to! Mind you, I did occasionally feel the wrath of the Headmaster's cane. He was called 'Porky' Davies, a rugby league fanatic, who had begun teaching at Grange Park School in Thatto Heath.

My sport developed nicely. My academic career did not and I used to receive the customary clip round the ear from my dad when the reports went home. At Parr, I played both rugby league and football at town and representative level. How I fitted everything in is amazing when I come to think of it. I didn't really know what I would do after I had left school, but to play sport at any level was an absolute must! At Parr we had Syd Green, who was pretty high up in football administration who took teams and, believe it or not, my skills on the left wing were brought to the attention of Derby County, who were managed by Clough and Taylor. I imagined I would be like their own left winger Alan Hinton, who wore distinctive white boots. But it was only preliminary interest and nothing came of it.

There was a lad a few years ahead of me in the town football team called Tommy O'Neill, who was a terrific sportsperson. He could have signed for Saints, but ended up playing for Manchester United at right back. Perhaps that was a situation I would have liked to have been in, but he was exceptional.

4

IKE FISHWICK

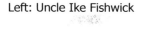
Left: Uncle Ike Fishwick

Meanwhile, in my early days at Parr, there was actually one sporting activity that I truly hated: swimming! Our teacher was Jeff Hitchen, who had played for Saints in the mid–1960s after signing from St Helens RUFC and he was getting a bit fed up with a few of us conveniently forgetting our trunks. One time I tried to pull the usual trick and he said: "You're going in next week – trunks or no trunks"! Come the day at the baths [bolted on to our school, incidentally] my mate Steve Brennan and I said we had once again forgotten our trunks. To cut a long story short, he threw us both in the pool with no trunks on.

Unfortunately for Mr. Hitchen, the punishment back-fired a little. The girls were in next lesson and he had to go and provide towels to hide our modesty as they were lining up waiting to use the pool. Mr Hitchen once decided I would never make it as a rugby league player. Needless to say in the ensuing years I was so glad to prove him wrong! Perhaps that's why he said it, you never know. It was great psychology.

As I went through the years at Parr, I was still captain of football and rugby league at school and town level. I was a hooker in league and a strolling left-winger in the round ball game. Incidentally, two lads at the time from our rivals St Cuthbert's actually made the grade with Manchester City: Gary Owen [midfield] and Ray Ranson, who was a full-back. Although the prospect of playing for a big football club obviously appealed to me, I became really 'into' my rugby. After all, that's the direction I wanted to go to follow in the footsteps of my uncles. The physical nature of the game certainly seemed to suit me and I thought I had the skills to succeed. I wanted to make as big an impression in the game as my hero from the terraces, Doug Laughton – and it became my burning ambition to wear the red and white jersey of my home town team, the Saint. After captaining teams throughout my school years and playing representative rugby, including captaining Lancashire schoolboys at Under–16s, it was not out of the question. My parents, as usual, were extremely supportive and would back me in whatever I wanted to do. In

5

fact, I would describe my dad as my biggest fan and critic. He was always there in the good and not so good times, without question.

Post-school days

If I was to succeed in rugby league, which was a semi-professional sport, I would still need a job. I left school at 16, without too many qualifications – apart from my sporting achievements. It was difficult at that stage. Initially I wanted to be a brick-layer, but one of my first jobs was at Burtonwood brewery in the bottle store. I wanted a job that would help me to keep fit, so handling crates and barrels was good for me to develop my strength. Then, uncle Bill helped me to get a job with the local corporation, as part of a pipe-laying gang. This involved digging trenches and replacing water supply pipes and drains. I remember when our boss, Mr Tushingham, came to visit us on site, he always seemed to be having a go at me, in a good-natured way. "Harry...every time I come to see you, you are always on top of the trench! Any chance of seeing you actually *in* the trench for a change"? My response was always the same: "I'm saving these hands for rugby league."

That is what I wanted, but I wasn't actually playing for anyone when I left school, although I did play cricket at Sutton CC as a wicket-keeper. Ray Howard, a Saints' player, who played at Rainhill CC at the time put in a few good words for me down at St Helens RFC. Like I said, it was always my ambition to play for St Helens and my big break was to come when I was invited to join the Colts team at Knowsley Road. Bob Dagnall, a Saints great and a hooker like my uncle Ike, was in charge of the team, with his friend Johnny Fishwick, who had played for Rochdale Hornets.

We played our home games at Merton Bank and rarely played at Knowsley Road in any curtain-raisers. We played all the top clubs, like Wigan, Warrington and Widnes, although our matches with Wigan were always 'tasty' affairs. I did well, early on and did enough to enable the club to sign me on professional forms. It really was a dream come true! It was done under the gaze of chairman Harry Cook, first team coach Eric Ashton, Colts coach Bob Dagnall and my dad. Three other lads signed on at the same time: Tommy Cunningham, Mike Nolan and Johnny Smith. We had our photographs taken later on in our kit, but it might have been in cherry and white! Wigan had shown an interest in me, initially, but backed off in the end because they thought I was too small! Despite Wigan's reservations, I settled down to play some good games in the Colts and looked forward to the next step with the 'A' team. One step before the seniors.

HARRY'S FAMILY

HARRY PINNER as you've never seen him before! These "exclusive" family album photographs include the Knowsley Road pack ace as a bouncing baby and as the proud young fisherman with dad Harold. Harry's mum Connie is also in focus and there's chance to see Harry as a youngster with sister Pat.

● *A FUTURE Saints skipper rarin' to go.*

● *THE Curly Kid ...*

● *HAPPY family days at the seaside.*

● *SMILES all round with sister Pat.*

● *"LISTEN here Harry, I'm playing acting half-back".*

7

FLASHBACKS

What a set of Likely Lads!

• CAN you spot the future international among this set of Likely Lads?

• HARRY, already showing off a strapping build in his paddling days.

• "BE patient Harry!" Harry seems to be losing faith in dad's fishing ability.

• BOY Wonder! Pinner, the chunky youngster who developed into the complete player.

• NICE work lad! Harry, Saints player of the year 1979/80 lets Dad Harold share his glory.

PAGE THIRTY THREE

8

2. Dad's Army and the Young Gun

"As a schemer and runner Harry can be classed in the top bracket. He may not have the devastating defence of Karalius, but when next time you watch, take note of how much he has the ball and how much involved in the play he is."
Tommy Bishop

A willing apprentice

Duggie Laughton might have been my favourite player when I watched from the terraces at Knowsley Road, but for as long as I could remember, I wanted to follow in the footsteps of my Uncle Ike, who had been a successful hooker – or number nine as they call it these days. When I was in the Colts, however, there were two of us in contention for the hooking spot. Tommy Cunningham was the other guy, who was Eddie and Keiron's brother and, to cut a long story short, he was given the nine jersey by our Coaches Bob Dagnall and Johnny Fishwick and I was switched to loose forward. In the long term, it was the making of my career! Sorry Uncle Ike...it really was for the best!

In the 'A' Team in the mid–1970s were the usual combination of regular, solid players who could be called up to the seniors on occasions and the younger element, who were looking to make a name for themselves in the game. It was a tough environment for any young player and a real 'training ground' for what was to come if you wanted to progress into the first team. Despite the age difference, I thought that the senior lads genuinely appreciated what I could bring to the team and there was no obvious resentment. The 'A' Team at that time included players like Chris Charles, the former rugby union star from Wales, a huge man who seemed to find it quite difficult to settle into the 13-a-side game and Neil Courtney, a really tough front-rower who never took a backward step. He went on to play for Saints, Warrington and Wigan, before he had to finish through injury. There was Kenny Thompson, a tough centre; Ray Howard was one of the older players, a centre who was still quite quick; Dave Campbell, a speedy winger who could score some good tries, who went on to become a Grade One referee; Mike Nolan was a nippy stand-off, with Peter Glynn from Widnes on the verge of a breakthrough into the first team – a fantastic player on his day.

Keiron Pickavance was a strong-running forward who showed great promise in the Colts. We were quite friendly at the time and he had something that I hadn't got – a car! Tommy Cunningham came up with me from the Colts and was quite impressive. He was quick around the play-the-balls and very much like the 'number nines' of today in that respect. For a spell we had an Australian stand-off called Les Mara, who joined us short-term from Balmain. He was a really decent player and returned to Australia shortly after. Our coach was Billy Boycott, who was a really pleasant and helpful guy. Overall, as I said, it was a real step up in terms of toughness and I remember, on occasions, we would have some senior players in the opposition who were coming back from injury, like when we played Wigan 'A', who had Colin Clarke in their line-up. I was doing well, as the newspaper report below shows:

St Helens Newspaper and Advertiser
10 February 1976
Oldham 'A' 2 St Helens 'A' 17

"Saints 'A' gathered revenge for their cup semi-final defeat by Oldham 'A' with a brilliant display at Watersheddings on Saturday. Oldham's only points came from a penalty by Larder, but Saints hit back with a 70-yard try by Pinner, following good work by Thompson and Campbell. In the second half a kick through by Peter Glynn resulted in Thompson scoring and Pinner added the points. Pinner scored another brilliant try under the posts. The young loose forward converted his effort and landed two more penalties to inflict Oldham's first home defeat this season."

Breaking through

I felt as though a call-up for the seniors would soon be on the cards, although when I did get chosen, in the number 14 jersey for the game at Hull KR on 28 December 1975, I didn't get on. I was a non-playing substitute. It was frustrating, as the team won fairly easily, 18–4, although it isn't quite like today, when the bench is an interchange one and in most cases the subs will be on at some stage as part of the game plan. Perhaps it was Eric Ashton's way of giving me a taste of senior rugby and not bringing me on too quickly.

I kept my head down and continued to do well in the 'A' team until another chance came: selection as substitute for the game against Dewsbury on 9 March 1976. I really did think I would get onto the field this time, although I was wrong. It was a really tight game at Crown Flatt and perhaps Eric didn't really want to make a change to possibly disrupt the flow of the match. I had to wait until later that month to make my actual debut on the field, a straight selection at loose forward for the game against Wakefield Trinity at Knowsley Road. This was what I had dreamed about for all those years, running out through the tunnel with many of the lads who I used to watch on the terraces. But it was a fantastic experience. You can see why they were called Dad's Army at the time, as the average age of the team was 28; I was the youngest at

19, with six players over the age of 30: Geoff Pimblett, Billy Benyon, Frank Wilson, Jeff Heaton, John Mantle and Tony Karalius.

As it happened, it was not the best of debuts, as we lost 10–7 to Trinity, after leading 7–6 at half-time. Their full-back Henry Oulton had a good day with the boot, but I don't think we did ourselves any favours. It was our third successive home defeat, which meant that our hopes of retaining the First Division title were slipping. Even so, I thought it was a brilliant experience for me – not the result – and, of course, I wanted to establish myself in that number 13 jersey.

On the bench that day as substitute forward was Graham Liptrot, who had made his debut in the first team several years before. In his sixth game, he was a member of the team that beat the Australian tourists at Knowsley Road. Not many can say that! The week after my debut for Saints I was with the Great Britain Colts team in France.

The Saints' team for my full debut was: Geoff Pimblett (2 goals), Les Jones, Billy Benyon, Derek Noonan, Roy Mathias (1 try), Frank Wilson, Jeff Heaton; John Mantle, Tony Karalius, Mel James, Eric Chisnall, Dave Hull, Harry Pinner. Subs: Ken Gwilliam, Graham Liptrot.

It was a fantastic team to make my debut in and one that contained some all-time great Saints' players, even if the average age was perhaps into the early 30s. At full-back, Geoff Pimblett was so cool under pressure. He was a great goalkicker, courageous for his size and joined the line well in attack. On the wings were Les Jones and Roy Mathias. Local lad Les was strong, quick and a good finisher; Roy was strong and direct. Few opposition wingers wanted to tackle him. He was quite big for a winger at the time, although I believe he had played in the back row when he played rugby union in Wales. Not many got past Derek Noonan at left centre. What he lacked in pace he made up for in guile and courage. On the right was Billy Benyon and I could never praise him enough. A good footballer; hard and courageous, who led by example. He had a great 'man-and-ball' tackle and when he became coach years later, he proved himself to be a good motivator. At stand-off for the Wakefield game was Frank Wilson, who normally played in the backs. He was very elusive and a good all-round player. I don't think he knew what he was going to do himself at times and certainly was unpredictable. Jeff Heaton was a typical solid scrum-half, similar to Warrington's Parry Gordon. A real grafter, although he lacked a bit of pace.

The pack included John Mantle and Mel James in the front-row. John had been a hard-running second-rower, but had started to play more up front. He did what he had to do; he had no fear and was well-respected by everyone. Welshman Mel was quiet off the field but on it, he never took a backward step. Mel was 'first man in' during his career and always drove the ball in hard. Mel once had a bit of a 'do' with Mal Reilly when we played Castleford and he didn't like it. Mal went around bashing as

11

many of our forwards as he could afterwards, although as a youngster, he left me alone.

At hooker was Tony Karalius, a magic ball-handler and a typical 'old time' hooker who knew all the tricks of the trade. Eric Chisnall and Dave Hull made up the back row that day. Eric was strong, could run and was a good club man. Dave played hard and was a really solid runner and tackler. He had played mostly at 'loose' and I think it was the first time he had played in the second-row. Competition between us for the 13 jersey would be intense.

On the bench was Ken Gwilliam, another hard-grafting scrum-half and my mate Graham Liptrot, who had played in the 'A' team before me. Regular hooker Tony Karalius was nearing the end of his career at Knowsley Road and Graham looked to be his obvious successor. We both wanted to be 'cemented' into the first team at some stage and both had high hopes of doing that in the foreseeable future.

One thing that is different from today is the sheer number of games played. All told, Saints played 52 senior competitive matches in the 1975–76 season. There was the League, Lancashire Cup, Player's No.6 Trophy, BBC 2 Floodlit Trophy, Challenge Cup and Premiership to play for. The team had already lifted the Floodlit Trophy and by the time I had made my debut, were preparing for a third round Challenge Cup tie with Oldham at Watersheddings. If we won, Wembley was on the horizon. 17–9 saw us into the semi-finals against Keighley and odds-on favourites to get to the Twin Towers. In fact, my second game for the seniors was against Keighley, at Knowsley Road. They were relegation candidates. We won 21–2 and I was pleased with my performance, especially when I was named 'Man of the Match':

St Helens Newspaper and Advertiser, 23 March 1976
Chris Hart reports:
"Saints showed they have strength in depth when six reserves helped them end a sequence of three successive defeats in the league, increasing Keighley's relegation worries and creating doubts over their survival in the Challenge Cup. Top of the lot was Man of the Match loose forward Harry Pinner, playing only his second senior game and, at 19 years, he must be one of the most exciting young prospects to emerge from the junior ranks at Knowsley Road for many years."

My third game for the seniors was the league game at Watersheddings, on 20 March, when a few changes had been made from the cup tie squad. I was at loose forward with some of the other 'A' Team lads, Mick Hope and Billy Platt in the second row. Ken Thompson and Chris Charles were also on the bench. We won 15–8. It was a difficult time for Eric Ashton because we faced a total of 15 matches in less than two months, with our involvement in cups and various postponements from earlier on in the season.

Despite that, I did not see myself being called up just yet for the big matches, unless there was a really bad injury list. I remember being presented with our medals after winning the Lancashire Combination and I had really enjoyed the experience of playing 'A' team football. I was also doing the goalkicking and at one point near the end of the season I had kicked nearly 80 goals in 21 matches.

We won the league by five points, with Wigan in second place and also we were by far the leading scorers in the competition. I also was part of the squad that played in the Headingley Sevens, when we beat some big names from Bradford Northern, in the first game, only to fall to a brilliant Salford team in the next round. What was a big boost was to be included in the squad which went to Wembley as 18th man. I think it was Eric Ashton's way of wanting to give me experience of the big occasion so that I was meant to feel one of the squad. We stayed at Cobham and I remember we had problems finding a pitch to train on. Club secretary Geoff Sutcliffe had to search for a pitch after two rugby union clubs turned us down. Even though we were only reserves, 'Lippy' and I were on the bench in just our tracksuits as our 'ageing' team beat Widnes in the scorching heat. Then it was a Premiership Final, against Salford two weeks later, but this time my hopes had been raised when I was named as substitute with Ken Gwilliam for the game at Swinton. I was disappointed not to come on, but we won 15–2, after being 1–0 down at half-time. George Nicholls was brilliant, as was another lad who came up through the ranks with me, Peter Glynn. He scored a try as he did in the Wembley final, although he began the game at centre, not from the bench like he did in London. Although I didn't get on, it was still a winner's medal at top level and the Saints had won the double.

Dad's Army's final fling?

The 1975–76 season was the last for some really great players at Saints, such as skipper Kel Coslett, John Mantle and scrum-half Jeff Heaton. The average age of the team remained high, with Billy Benyon appointed captain for 1976–77 and other legends who were into their 30s, such as Tony Karalius, Geoff Pimblett and my mentor, George Nicholls. I did think I had a good chance of becoming an established senior player. I had done well at the 'back end' of the season – selected 12 times; played on nine occasions – had played Colts' international rugby for Great Britain and coach Eric Ashton seemed to rate me highly. We trained twice a week, with the first and 'A' teams together. We would do a variety of running and sprinting including some 25 yard 'burst' sprints and finish off with a game of tick-and-pass.

13

Signing on: Four lads who have become fully-fledged Saints, with Colts' Coach Bob Dagnall: Mike Nolan, Johnny Smith, Tommy Cunningham, Harry Pinner. (Courtesy Harry Pinner)

Learning the trade: The Saints 'A' team in all its glory. Back: Harry Pinner, Billy Platt, Neil Courtney, Mike (Graham) Shaw, Chris Charles, Peter Glynn, Keiron Pickavance; front: Les Mara, Tommy Cunningham, Mike Nolan, Dave Campbell, Kenny Thompson, Roy Howard, Peter Brown. (Courtesy Bill Appleton)

14

St Helens RFC 1975–76: Back: Harry Pinner, Graham Liptrot, Peter Glynn, George Nicholls, Mel James, Eric Chisnall, Billy Benyon, David Hull, John Mantle; Middle row: Geoff Pimblett, Les Jones, Jeff Heaton, Kel Coslett (Capt), Roy Mathias, Derek Noonan, Eddie Cunningham; front: Ken Thompson, Frank Wilson, Ken Gwilliam, Tony Karalius. (Courtesy Harry Pinner)

The bench at Wembley salutes Jeff Heaton's try in the 1976 Challenge Cup final. Graham Liptrot (right) and Billy Benyon are next to Harry. Coach Eric Ashton (in front of Harry) manages to hide his obvious delight. (Courtesy Alex Service)

Occasionally, I would want to do 'extras' and dad would pick me up and I would return home to do some weights. My bedroom was my improvised gym. If not I would have a drink with the rest of the lads at the Black Bull before going back.

My usual pre-match routine is certainly different from those of today's full-time professionals. For a Friday night game at Knowsley Road, I would get back from work and have beans or egg on toast – basically something light. I would go down to the ground and get ready, get strapped and maybe have a rub-down. Physio Ken Henthorne and a few others were always available for this. Unfortunately, one of the things I used to do was to wretch before a game, just before we were due to go onto the field. It was just nerves and it had become normal since my 'A' team days. My mum used to make steak and eggs, originally, but she thought it was an expensive waste of a good steak every week with my 'nervous habit' so egg on toast it was. We did a few stretches when we went onto the field, but that was the extent of our warm up.

After the game, any injuries would be treated with ice and Doc Lomax would be on hand to assess any of the more serious knocks – perhaps a big contrast from the professional rugby league environment of today.

It was interesting that the 1976–77 season kicked off with Saints getting all the wrong headlines. We drew Wigan in the first round of the Lancashire Cup at Central Park and were smashed 37–5, with Wigan winger Green Vigo scoring five tries. It wasn't the best of starts, but there was an explanation. Our team was severely weakened as a result of a players' strike. It was basically an 'A' team, with most of the lads included who had helped to win the Lancashire Combination he previous year. We also lost our second game, at Rochdale. It was the first time we faced our former skipper Kel Coslett and Jeff Heaton. We drew in the third against Wakefield at home 7–7, but gradually got into our stride.

Despite the changes in the squad, the Saints were still one of the most powerful teams in the league and I was hoping to play a big part in the 1976–77 season. What happened certainly exceeded my expectations. I played 36 matches – the team played 44 overall – and shared in the team's journey to the Challenge Cup semi-finals and the Premiership Trophy Final. We finished runners up in the league and most people would fail in a quiz to name the top team – Featherstone Rovers, who finished with 44 points from 30 matches, five points more than us. I also continued to be selected for representative games, made my debut for Lancashire in the County Championship and graduated from the Colts to the Great Britain Under–24s, who played the French twice.

Top teams have a good representation in the scorers' lists and for the Saints it was Eddie Cunningham with 26 tries, a strong centre or second rower who was so difficult to tackle and Roy Mathias, who had become one of the most dangerous wingers in the First Division, who ran in 23.

Geoff Pimblett came second in the goalkicking charts to Castleford's Sammy Lloyd with 152 and was another experienced player who made such a difference to us.

Climbing the international ladder

It was a natural progression from the Colts to Under 24s level, although much tougher. I was proud to make my debut on 14 November against the French at Hull KR's Craven Park at loose forward, with Hull's Jimmy Crampton and Salford's Sammy Turnbull in the back row. Our opponents had a strong group from Carcassonne, including my opposite number, Joel Roosbrouck, who was a superb player. Keith Mumby kicked five goals and we won comfortably 19–2 in front of a good crowd of just over 6,000. The RFL had scrapped this level in 1969, so I was playing in the first game after its re-introduction. It is interesting to see the Great Britain line-up from that day. Not all that many of the team graduated to full test match level. I was lucky to do so later on, together with Mumby, Mike Smith, Dickinson, Eddie Szymala, Hall and David Ward.

Under–24 International
Great Britain (19) 19 France (0) 2
Sunday 14 November 1976
Craven Park, Hull.

Great Britain: Mumby (Bradford Northern 5G); Muscroft (New Hunslet), Roe (Bradford Northern), M. Smith (Hull KR), D. Smith (Leeds 1T); Burton (Castleford), Nulty (Wigan 1T); Dickinson (Leeds), Szymala (Barrow), Wood (Widnes), Crampton (Hull), Turnbull (Salford 1T), Pinner (St Helens) Subs: Hall (Hull KR), Ward (Leeds)
France: Guigue (Avignon); Sire (Catalan), Dumas (Lezignan), Guilhem (Carcassonne), Chauvet (Carcassonne); Valligonda (Lezignan 1G), Alard (Carcassonne); Fratini (Marseille), Bonet (Avignon), Cassin (Toulouse), Beraudo (Avignon), Caravaca (Carcassonne), Roosebrouk (Villeneuve) Subs: Laville (Villeneuve), Mayorgas (Toulouse)
Referee: Mick Naughton [Widnes]
Attendance: 6,086

On 5 December there was the return at Albi and we knew it was going to be a more difficult match. The French referee was Monsieur Auriolle from Toulouse and it was difficult to get any decisions to go our way. I kicked a drop-goal which, I suppose, helped us to win 11–9. Peter Roe and David Smith scored our tries. But rugby was second to outright thuggery. It was an awful experience as we had to endure constant provocation from our opponents during and after the match.

17

Great Britain Under-24s versus France at Hull 14 November 1976. This was the first match for this age group. Note the 'lace up' Adidas jerseys.
Back: Roy Dickinson (Leeds), Peter Muscroft (New Hunslet), Jimmy Crampton (Hull), Sammy Turnbull (Salford), David Smith (Leeds), Mike Smith (Hull KR), David Hall (Hull KR), John Wood (Widnes), Peter Roe (Bradford Northern); front: Johnny Whiteley (Coach), Jimmy Nulty (Wigan), Harry Pinner (St Helens), Bruce Burton (Castleford, Captain), Harry Womersley (Team Manager), David Ward (Leeds), Eddie Syzmala (Barrow), Keith Mumby (Bradford Northern), John Williams (Physio). (Courtesy *Rugby League Journal*)

To show how bad it was, our hooker, Eddie Szymala was approached by a member of the opposition and he seemed to want to swap jerseys. When Eddie started to take his jersey off for the proposed swap, he received a kick, shall we say, where it hurts. They were awful that day. It has always been remembered as the 'Battle of Albi' for those reasons.

Pride of the Red Rose

The County Championship had been going for many years and arguably was on its last legs. Crowds were disappointing, but it was still regarded as a top representative honour and a stepping stone to further selection at international level. I was first selected for Lancashire for the game against Cumbria on 2 February at Leigh. Although I was the only Saints' player picked for either side, I didn't get on the pitch and had the dreaded 'dnp' after my name on the final team sheet. Lancashire's back three that Wednesday night included Leigh's Tommy Martyn (father of stand-off Tommy junior who played for Saints), Mick Adams of Widnes and Dennis Boyd, also of Leigh. We won 18–14, but it was obviously frustrating to be on the bench.

Fortunately, I did get on a few weeks later when we played Yorkshire at Castleford, when I replaced Dennis Boyd. We lost 18–13 and Yorkshire won the competition, courtesy of their drawn game against Cumbria.

Looking at the two teams, there are some really excellent players taking part. These county games were, in their own way, a real test trial and enabled me to test my mettle against some really top players, like Dave Topliss, David Ward and the Hull KR duo, Paul Rose and Phil Lowe. Also my opposite number was the great 'Knocker' Norton, then of Castleford and our paths were to cross many times over the next few years at club and representative level.

County Championship

Yorkshire (3) 18 Lancashire (10) 13
Tuesday 1 March 1977
Wheldon Road, Castleford.
Lancashire: Fairbairn (Wigan 3G), Fielding (Salford), Hughes (Widnes 1T), Hesford (Warrington), Wright (Widnes), Gill (Salford), Bowden (Widnes), Hodkinson (Rochdale Hornets), Elwell (Widnes 1DG), Wood (Widnes), Martyn (Warrington 1T), Adams (Widnes), Boyd (Leigh). Subs: Aspey (Widnes), Pinner (St Helens)
Yorkshire: Mumby (Bradford Northern 1G), Muscroft (New Hunslet 1T), Crook (Wakefield Trinity), Francis (Wigan), Atkinson (Leeds), Topliss (Wakefield Trinity), Stephens (Castleford), Thompson (Featherstone Rovers), Ward (Leeds 1T), Farrar (Featherstone Rovers), Rose (Hull KR 1T), Lowe (Hull KR), Norton (Castleford). Subs: N. Stephenson (Dewsbury 1T), Lloyd (Castleford 2G).
Referee: P. Massey (Salford)
Attendance: 2,740

It was brilliant to be picked on merit each week and accepted by far more experienced players, which is not always the case when a new face comes in. In this respect, I cannot over-emphasise the help given to me in particular by George Nicholls. He was a real mentor to me and I cannot thank him enough for his help and advice. The lads seemed to have confidence in my ability and I certainly did not feel over-awed in their company. We got over the initial rumblings over the players' strike and settled down into what was the usual busy season. As I said, the number of competitions is so unlike today and you needed strength in depth if you were going to succeed. Players played more with knocks then. If they didn't they wouldn't get paid and it was always nice to bring home that winning bonus, especially away from home.

Our home record was good. We only lost two, including Wigan on Boxing Day, 14–12, and an amazing game against Castleford in the John Player trophy, covered by the BBC, when we were cruising 18–5 at half-time and they came back to win 22–18. One of our best wins was 9–4 at Wigan in the Challenge Cup third round, although our hopes of retaining the Challenge Cup disappeared against Leeds in the semi-final at Wigan. We lost a tight game 7–2. Leeds went on to beat Widnes in the final.

19

But this game still rankles with me. George Nicholls withdrew because of flu, which didn't help. About 20 minutes into the match we did a set-piece move. I booted the ball up as high as I could and Geoff Pimblett was supposed to chase and, hopefully get a try. This worked like a dream, only for referee Fred Lindop to disallow it for offside. Geoff was a smart player; he had timed his run to perfection and was way onside. He was really upset about it as well and I don't blame him. It was a really close game; that decision cost us the match and our hold on the Challenge Cup. We just had to accept it. Referees in those days were all different characters although we knew what to expect from each one. Today, they tend to be bland and don't have the same intimacy with the players. Only the captain can talk to the referee. We didn't have the screens they have to make decisions in the televised games. I think that they are over-used. Referees are under increasing pressure and need to be extra sure of their decisions. Wrong decisions can mean they are stood down. A few would have been stood down in my day, for sure!

The Premiership Trophy was another piece of silverware that we could retain, although we began with a draw at home to Wigan in round 1, 10–10 and won the replay 8–3. The semi-finals were over two legs and we won both matches against Castleford to reach the final with Warrington. It was tight in the first half and we were 5–4 down before coming through after the break to win 32–20. Geoff Pimblett won the Harry Sunderland trophy after another brilliant game for us. It was the first silverware that I had earned with a full appearance. But there was a twist. I was sent off after clashing with Warrington's scrum-half Alan Gwilliam. He was having a good game and we ended up having a bit of a set-to. When we got sent off there was some crowd trouble behind the goal and the fans pelted each other with fragments of the railway sleepers from the terracing. Opposing fans clashing was not unheard of in those days. Because as I had been dismissed, I could not go up with the team to receive my medal at the end, which was disappointing. But we had a good time back at Knowsley Road at the club's buffet.

Premiership Trophy Final
St Helens (4) 32 Warrington (5) 20
Saturday 28 May 1977, Station Road, Swinton.
St Helens: Pimblett (1T 7G), Jones, Benyon (1T), Cunningham (1T), Mathias (1T), Glynn, K. Gwilliam (1T), D. Chisnall, Liptrot, James (1T), Nicholls, E. Chisnall, Pinner. Subs: Ashton, Karalius
Warrington: Finnigan, Curling, Bevan, Hesford (4G), Kelly, A. Gwilliam (1T), Gordon (1T), Weavill (1T), Price, Case, Lester, Martyn, Philbin (1T) Subs: Peers, Cunliffe
Harry Sunderland Trophy: Geoff Pimblett (St Helens)
Referee: F. Lindop (Wakefield)
Attendance: 11,507

3. Great entertainers at Wembley

"Young Pinner, for a forward, has probably come on faster than any other I've ever known. It's been taking us all our time to hold him back and, for his age, he is going like a bomb. I rate Pinner a great prospect. He is very keen, is always willing to listen to advice and wants to succeed with highly commendable urgency."
Eric Ashton

I really looked forward to the 1977–78 season. Although I was now toothless in the literal sense, – too much collateral damage over the years – I hoped that the Saints would continue to have some 'bite' during the forthcoming matches. I was first choice loose forward and really settling into a Saints team that would always be in contention for honours – and winning money was quite plentiful. Apart from Peter Glynn, Graham Liptrot and me, the team was generally an experienced one. It contained a number of the so-called Dad's Army lads from 1976, such as full-back Geoff Pimblett, who had taken over as captain from his good friend Kel Coslett. Geoff was still a superb player and played in 42 of the 48 matches. He kicked 159 goals, including 13 when we beat Bramley 71–7 at Knowsley Road.

George Nicholls was a tower of strength in the pack and got even better as the season went along. Dave Chisnall was in his second season with us and his power, experience and mobility for a big man gave our pack a formidable look. Derek Noonan also entered his second season at Knowsley Road and made more appearances than anyone else, 45, and was a brilliant defender out wide at centre.

Bill Francis was a key signing from Wigan. Some say that he was past his best, but he was great for my own game and kept the line moving with his superb passes. He also was elusive with a brilliant body swerve. Another vital member of our team was Eddie Cunningham, who could play centre or second row and was so difficult to knock down with his bull-like strength. He was leading try-scorer with 29 and our wingers Les Jones and Roy Mathias scored 45 between them. Our total of tries for the season was 218 and we got a bit of a reputation as an entertaining side who were not afraid to give the ball some air. Being entertaining is one thing, but it does not necessarily mean winning trophies. A bit of steel and what they call today 'game management' plus a large slice of luck somewhere along the line to succeed is required.

In the first half of the season up to New Year, we won 12 out of 16 league matches. In the cups, we lost away to Featherstone Rovers in the John Player Trophy second round and were defeated 5–4 by Workington Town in the Lancashire Cup semi-final at Derwent Park.

St Helens 20 Featherstone Rovers 19 on 10 December 1977 at Knowsley Road
Harry scored two tries in this match, in front of just 2,800 fans.

We did reach the BBC2 Floodlit Trophy Final, but lost 26–11 in an entertaining game to Hull KR at Craven Park. It was a double whammy, because we returned to Craven Park five days later in the league and lost again, 21–9.

Perhaps it is true to say that I had not been in tip-top form in the early part of the 1977–78 season and this was reflected in my relegation to the bench for Great Britain Under-24s against France at Hull. Keith Bell of Featherstone Rovers came in. Looking through my cuttings, an article by Arthur Brooks in the *Daily Mirror* on 11 November 1977 probably summed up my progress at the time: "Harry Pinner has just the right initials for putting plenty of spice into his game....and this classy loose-forward does just that for St Helens. HP is just 21, a Young Lion of immense dedication to this tough game of rugby league and substitute forward for the Great Britain U24 team facing France at Hull Tomorrow. Relegation to substitute has been a bit of a blow to Harry, who featured prominently in our U24 side's devastating double over the French at Hull and Albi last season.

'Naturally I am a little upset at not keeping a firm grip on that number 13 jersey,' says Harry, a pipe-layer and bachelor who lives at Sutton, St Helens. 'I expect it's because I lost some of my form at the start of this season and, now that I've recovered it, I suppose I should be grateful to be in the squad.'

"It's confidently expected that Great Britain Under-24 coach Johnny Whiteley will play Harry at some stage of tomorrow's battle at the Boulevard. For in Harry Pinner he knows he has an ace up his sleeve – a fierce-tackling, hard-running and slick ball distributing forward, who never lets his club or country down. Harry five feet 10½ inches tall and tipping the scales at 13 stone, who went marching in with Saints from their Colts team three years ago, used to be worried at his slight lack of weight and height in that vital number 13 berth. But he has turned out to be a pocket battleship of a loose forward, has altered his style of play under the guidance of St Helens ace coach Eric Ashton and has matured rapidly. 'I was worried at one stage about not being heavy enough, but I'm slowly putting the pounds on now and reckon I'll be at my ideal weight when in 13 stone 10 pounds' Harry told me. 'Gradually, I've moulded my own style of play and have started specialising in a more individualist role.'"

Really, my play was bound to improve through being behind one of the finest second rowers in the business in George Nicholls, who encouraged me so much over the years.

We beat the French quite comfortably at Hull, 27–9, and I did get on, for second-rower Trevor Skerrett, and scored a try. My good friend Graham Liptrot was hooking and dominated the scrums, so it was a good night all round for us. Leigh's John Woods at stand-off also played well.

The French seemed to have had a much-changed team for the return at Tonneins just before Christmas and, predictably it was much harder to get the win. We really did have to work hard for our 8–4 victory. Once again I came on from the bench for another second-rower, Mick Gibbins. Unlike the previous season, I didn't feature for Lancashire, or for England in the European Championship, which was disappointing. Len Casey and 'Knocker' Norton were the two loose forwards in the England matches.

The second half of the season was generally good for us. From January onwards we played 22 matches in all competitions and lost just four. Our progress in the Challenge Cup began with a defeat of Huyton at home, followed by a potentially difficult match at Watersheddings against Oldham, which we won 26–11. The following week we beat Huddersfield at home and looked forward to the semi-final against Warrington, coached by Alex Murphy, who were always difficult opponents. The game drew over 16,000 to Wigan and we eventually won 12–8, but it was a really close game. Our forwards played well, including Mel James and Dave Chisnall, but the real star was George Nicholls, who was everywhere it seemed. He did one tackle on John Bevan which kept us in the game because it looked like a try was very much on. I put a high kick up for our first try, which was palmed back to me by Ken Gwilliam. I then put the ball wide for Roy Mathias to score in the corner. Geoff Pimblett put over a brilliant conversion. Warrington got back in it with a try from Dalgreen, but I popped over a drop-goal on the half-hour to give us back the lead.

Just before half-time, Bevan scored in the corner for Warrington and then they had a try disallowed for a forward pass, which apparently was quite a controversial call. We got back ahead again when I linked with Ken Gwilliam and we got Eddie Cunningham away, who drew several defenders and passed to Mathias for his second. It was then 11–8 with another great touchline conversion from Pimblett. I kicked another one-pointer shortly afterwards and had another one disallowed for a Warrington touch. I tried another one in injury time and was belted by John Dalgreen, but it was worth it to reach Wembley. We had just about deserved it and Graham Liptrot won the scrums 2–1 to give us a big advantage. Even though the final was seven games away, the same side that played in the semi-final turned out at Wembley.

We wanted to possibly make it a double celebration, with the Premiership rounds before Wembley. We beat Salford comfortably at home and faced a two-legged semi-final against Bradford Northern. The first leg at Knowsley Road ended 14–10 for us. At Odsal, we had a dream start and led 8–4, which then became 12–5 with two drop-goals and a penalty from Pimblett. Things went downhill for us, though, when their big pack, with Ian van Bellen, Jim Thompson and Dennis Trotter, started to fire. In the end, they got to a single point of our aggregate lead, before Mumby kicked a penalty and Neil Fox and John Walford kicked drop-goals. The score ended 19–12; the aggregate 29–26. Perhaps there were lessons there for us, but the focus was now on Wembley and a dream final against Leeds, who had beaten Featherstone Rovers at Odsal.

Wembley here we come

Unlike the 1972 and 1976 finals, when I was a spectator, it was now my task to ensure that my family all got tickets: mum and dad, fiancée Wendy, her brother Alan, my sister Pat and her husband Phil. I had met Wendy at Saints – where else – when she and her friends used to come up to watch the games and marriage was on the cards in the near future.

In the *Daily Express* before the game, in an article by Jack Bentley I was quoted as saying: "We have the players to win, both in the forwards and the backs where I think we're faster than Leeds. As for me not being big enough for loose forward, I used to worry about it. But now I've played against bigger loose forwards, I'd rather have my extra yard of pace than an extra half-stone in weight."

The pack only had one survivor from when the team last played at Wembley: George Nicholls. He was struggling with a bit of a shoulder problem but there was no danger of him not playing. In the *Daily Express* Wembley special he spoke about my progress: "I have tried to help any of the lads I could. As for Harry, I found at first that he trying to do too much off his own bat. So I had a few chats with him. The great thing about Harry is that he will listen. And he is a good player now." Reading this, from one of my heroes, gave me a huge boost for the Big Day.

St Helens 12 Warrington 8, Challenge Cup semi-final 1978: Putting up a bomb as Warrington hooker John Dalgreen comes charging in. Geoff Pimblett (left) and Mel James are also in the picture. (Courtesy *Rugby League Journal*)

St Helens RFC Wembley squad 1978: Back: Geoff Pimblett, Les Jones, Eric Chisnall, George Nicholls, Derek Noonan, Mike Hope; third row: Eddie Cunningham, Harry Pinner, Graham Liptrot, Dave Chisnall, Neil Courtney; second row: Tony Karalius, Alan Ashton, Billy Benyon, Peter Glynn, Ken Gwilliam; front: Mel James, David Hull, Roy Mathias. (Courtesy Alex Service)

The *Daily Mirror* pre-Wembley article on 9 May 1978 said: "Pinner – a pipe-layer by trade – started marching in with Saints from their Colts team four years ago. And this season he has had 21 tries as a reward for his hard-running play and eagerness to cash in on every half chance. Harry is to be married in September to pretty, dark-haired Wendy Cowell, 22, an office worker. They have just bought a bungalow on the outskirts of St Helens. Bumper winnings from the Final would also go some way to buying furniture. 'I'm thoroughly enjoying my game and I'm alongside some tremendous players,' Harry told me. 'I'm also lucky, for I've got age on my side.' This specialist in breath-taking short but devastating bursts reckons his play has come on a ton since the arrival of international Bill Francis from Wigan. 'I'm coming off him well and he slings out a peach of a pass,' says Harry. 'I'm absolutely itching to get cracking at Wembley. It can't come soon enough for me and our squad is perfectly tuned-up for the big occasion. I consider we've an excellent chance of pulling it off... and possibly by 15 points to 8.'"

I was paired with Mick Crane at loose forward. In an article in the *Daily Mail*, Brian Batty asked Great Britain coach Johnny Whiteley about our abilities. This is what he came up with:

Mick Crane: "He plays a roaming, running game, which takes him out wide and makes him difficult to pick up."

Harry Pinner: "Harry plays closer to the pack. He works it tighter from the scrums, goes through with the short, sharp break and can dart and sidestep through the gaps."

The RFL love to have finals with a Lancashire-Yorkshire theme and there was a massive crowd, 95,872, as we came out before the kick-off to be introduced to the Earl of Derby. It was a terrific atmosphere that took our breath away. This is what every player wants to experience in their career. Deafening noise and flags flying all round the stadium. For Eric Ashton, it was his ninth appearance as a player (six) and a coach (three), so we knew from him exactly what to expect, but not every player can deal with it and the nerves are jangling until the match starts.

We started well and got Leeds on the back foot. After about four minutes, we scored an 'Australian' try in many ways. George Nicholls took it in and it was the last tackle. I was just inside the Leeds '25' and put up a high kick – or 'bomb' these days – which got quite a bit of height and drifted towards the right into the in-goal area. The Leeds full-back, Oulton tried to defuse it and the ball hit him on the chest. It then bounced off Atkinson almost right into the arms of Graham Liptrot, who touched down. It was a fantastic start and an easy conversion for Geoff Pimblett. It was a Saints try scored by St Helens lads and we enjoyed the moment.

Things got better for us around about 15 minutes. We had a scrum near Leeds's line and scrum-half Kenny Gwilliam passed to Bill Francis, who danced his way through a few attempted tackles for our second try.

26

St Helens 12 Leeds 14, Challenge Cup Final 1978

Trying desperately to get the attack moving: Stand-off Bill Francis is on the left.
(Courtesy Curtis Johnstone)

The killer blow: Leeds forward Phil Cookson takes three of us – Harry, Eddie
Cunningham and George Nicholls – over the line for the try that gave them the
momentum to win the match. (Courtesy Alex Service)

It was typical of Bill, who possessed some sensational attacking skills. Geoff Pimblett kicked the goal and at 10–0 we were flying. Our pack was on top and we were going well, with George Nicholls outstanding. They did manage to get on the scoreboard after twenty minutes, when they threw the ball wide out left. Les Dyl made the original break and he passed to Atkinson with thirty yards to go. It looked a bit forward, but he went on to beat Geoff Pimblett and my own desperate lunge nearly got him, but it was a fraction too late and he stumbled over in the corner. Oulton kicked the goal from out wide. But we didn't panic as such, especially when Geoff Pimblett put a penalty over to make it 12–5.

We sat in the dressing room at half time quietly confident. If Leeds wanted an open game, we could match them in all areas. In fact, the reverse happened. They had their big forwards playing down the middle at the restart and it certainly took it out of us. Straight after half-time David Ward dropped a goal to give them the first points and from a psychological point of view, it must have worked. Their forwards really took it out on us and they scored again after 55 minutes, when David Smith went over for a try but the conversion was missed. I seem to remember that Geoff Pimblett was narrowly wide with a drop-goal attempt with about a quarter of an hour to go which would have made it 13–9 and probably clinched it for us.

We still felt as though we were favourites, although with 10 minutes to go they made a crucial change by bringing on Roy Dickinson, another big forward, for Mick Harrison. It didn't seem long before John Holmes fed Cookson with a reverse pass. There was no stopping him and he forced his way over to level the game at 12–12. This is when we really felt under pressure. It was almost what they would call in Australia 'golden point' territory. A few minutes later we looked to have forced John Holmes out wide, but he managed to slot over a drop-goal with his weaker left foot. They got into our half again shortly after and we knew what was coming, but we couldn't stop David Ward getting his second one-pointer.

We didn't give up and nearly snatched it more or less on the final whistle when we attacked down the right. Peter Glynn gave Derek Noonan what looked like a try-scoring pass, but poor Derek spilled the ball with the line at his mercy. It was a gut-wrenching moment for him, but Leeds had dominated the game since half-time and we had difficulty in containing their big pack. We had no big forward, like Dickinson, to bring on and our substitutes, Alan Ashton and Tony Karalius, remained on the bench.

On a personal note, to lose at Wembley was an awful experience. Players never knew if they would ever be there again and, in my case, of course that would be true. We were so close and although it is seen as one of the greatest-ever finals, it was no consolation whatsoever. We were cheered up by the reaction of the fans when we came back to St Helens. They turned out in numbers and undoubtedly made us feel better, but it was so disappointing to return without the cup.

We played entertaining rugby and the Challenge Cup was by far our best chance for honours. We were beaten by being ground down as part of Leeds's second half game plan. Not to be derogative at all, but it's the sort of thing the likes of Kevin Sinfield would do to win a match today. We relied on our open football and of course could become a cropper.

Challenge Cup Final
St Helens (12) 12 Leeds (5) 14
Saturday 13 May 1978
Wembley Stadium, London.
St Helens: Pimblett (Capt 3G), Jones, Noonan, Glynn, Mathias, Francis (1T), K. Gwilliam, D. Chisnall, Liptrot (1T), James, Nicholls, Cunningham, Pinner. Subs: Ashton, Karalius
Leeds: Oulton (1G), D. Smith (1T), Hague, Dyl, Atkinson (1T), Holmes (1DG), Sanderson, Harrison, Ward (Capt 2DG), Pitchford, Eccles, Cookson (1T), Crane. Subs: Dick, Dickinson.
Lance Todd Trophy: George Nicholls (St Helens)
Referee: W. Thompson (Huddersfield)
Attendance: 95,872

I had thoroughly enjoyed the season as a whole despite the Wembley defeat. Overall, I had scored 21 tries, which was only just two short of Roy Mathias and Les Jones who both got 23. Peter Glynn, the 'Supersub' from 1976 scored 28, but our highest scorer was Eddie Cunningham, who got 30. This put him equal third in the overall charts, together with Warrington's John Bevan and Steve Fenton of Castleford. Stuart Wright of Widnes, who was the difference in the Floodlit Final against us, was top with 33. Keith Fielding was runner-up with 31. Geoff Pimblett topped the goalkickers' chart with 178 and was leading points scorer with 381.

After all that, it was time for other pressing matters. Wendy and I were married at Lowe House church in St Helens in September. My Best Man was our scrum-half, Alan Ashton and it was great to have my Uncle Bill there too, even though by then he was a bit unstable with his legs. We had our house ready in Paisley Avenue and looked forward to our new life together.

Dying embers of a great team

It always seemed that at the start of the season, we encountered problems and the 1978–79 campaign was no different. It took us three games to dispose of Rochdale Hornets in the first round of the Lancashire Cup, with the second replay at Central Park. Leigh beat us 21–4 at Hilton

Park in round two, but we lost only one game in September and October, although on 12 November, the visiting Australians gave us a real going-over, 26–4. They led 9–4 at half-time and we battered them for long spells, with the wind and rain at our backs, but couldn't force home an advantage.

Earlier, on 4 October, I had played for Great Britain Under-24s against them, at Hull. I came off the bench for Featherstone's Peter Smith but couldn't really make much of an impression. They certainly wanted some stopping and their threequarter line: Boustead, Rogers, Cronin, and Chris Anderson all scored tries. You couldn't really say that it was a mid-week 'ham and eggers' outfit. They had Bobby Fulton at stand-off and Tommy Raudonikis at seven – some great players there for sure. My opposite number was Parramatta legend Ray Price; Lippy had to face Canterbury's George Peponis, another top player, who was their captain. Even though we lost 30–8 it was a great experience for me to play in such company.

We didn't pick up much after the Kangaroo defeat, with five wins from eight into the New Year, including a 13–7 loss to Widnes at Knowsley Road in the final of the Floodlit Trophy. Duggie Laughton was at loose forward and it was their winger Stuart Wright who made the difference, with two tries. Mick Burke, who made his name more as a full-back played stand-off and scored a try. Widnes were becoming a strong side and would be right up there with the best of them by the early 1980s.

In the meanwhile, I had continued to feature for Lancashire and we won the County Championship on points difference from Yorkshire. In the first game, against Yorkshire at Widnes, I was on the bench with Peter Glynn and we both replaced Saints' players; I came on for George Nicholls, who was still very much on top of his game and Peter replaced Eddie Cunningham. To complete the St Helens connection, Bill Francis played at stand-off for Yorkshire. As for Lancashire, we had a Scot, Fairbairn, a Welshman – John Bevan – and Keith Fielding from the Midlands wearing the red and white hoops. They did score three tries and four goals between them I suppose as we hammered them 23–7.

A few weeks later, it was Cumbria at the Recreation Ground in Whitehaven. There was a large Saints' contingent, with Les Jones, Dave Chisnall, Graham Liptrot and George Nicholls in the starting line-up. I was on the bench with Peter Glynn and I came on for Eric Prescott, the former Saints' forward who had transferred to Salford, but we lost by a single point, 16–15. Iain MacCorquodale's five goals were probably the difference on the night for the Cumbrians, although it was always a difficult place to go to for a representative game in midweek.

There was a powerful second-row combination for Cumbria consisting of the Gorley brothers from Workington Town. In a few years both would be playing for Lancashire clubs, with great success.

The New Year saw us unbeaten in February and making good progress in the Challenge Cup. By the middle of March we had beaten Castleford 10–6 at Wheldon Road to march into the semi-finals. It was then that we struck a real loss of form. The following week we lost to Leeds at home and then the next three away matches. The last was Wakefield Trinity at Belle Vue, 23–3 on 1 April, the week before the Challenge Cup semi-final against the same opponents.

Eric Ashton felt as though he had to do something and left Geoff Pimblett out of the team, putting Peter Glynn at full-back. We made a good start and led 3–0 at the break after a fantastic Les Jones try. But they came at us strongly in the second half and won 9–7. Geoff announced his retirement after the game and it was another part of the break-up of the famous Dad's Army team. He finished with 105 goals and 201 points for the season. Roy Mathias with 22 and Peter Glynn with 19 were our top try-scorers. Our spekkies were used to seeing their team compete for the major trophies and although we did get to the Floodlit final, the Challenge Cup semi-final loss, to a team that finished five places below us in 10th place in the final league table, was a really bitter blow.

BBC2 Floodlit Trophy Final
St Helens (5) 7 Widnes (8) 13
Tuesday 12 December 1978
Knowsley Road, St Helens.
St Helens: Pimblett (2G), Jones, Glynn, Cunningham, Mathias, Francis, Holding, D. Chisnall (1T), Liptrot, James, Nicholls, Knighton, Pinner. Subs: Arkwright, E. Chisnall
Widnes: Eckersley, Wright (2T), Hughes, Aspey, P. Shaw, Burke (1T 2G), Bowden, Hogan, Elwell, Mills, Adams, Dearden, Laughton. Subs: J. Myler, G. Shaw
Referee: J. McDonald (Wigan)
Attendance: 10,250

Great Britain went on tour with Eric Ashton MBE at the helm. Perhaps the club had a moderate season by their previously high standards, but there were five Saints players chosen in the squad for Australia and New Zealand: Peter Glynn, Mel James, Roy Mathias, George Nicholls and my good mate Graham Liptrot. Naturally, I was disappointed at not being selected, but pleased for 'Lippy' who was a great hooker and would provide a capable understudy for David Ward. As it happened, George Nicholls was a nailed-on selection in all six tests against the Australians and the Kiwis, including some games in the front row. Roy Mathias played in the first test against Australia, at Lang Park and Peter Glynn was a non-playing substitute at Carlaw Park in the first match against New Zealand. Overall, New Zealand were beaten 2–1, but the Australians continued their dominance with a 3–0 whitewash. The first test against the Australians, at Lang Park was a disaster – a 35–0 defeat and Eric Ashton was absolutely devastated, but the damage was done. It seemed to make me more determined to be a part of the next tour, scheduled for 1984, but there would be a lot of water to flow under the bridge before that.

I was more determined than ever to continue my progress in top flight rugby league and I had the perfect tutor, the one-and-only Vince Karalius. I think he took an interest in my development because I was the number 13, just like he had been and wanted to give me any advice he could. When he was still living in Widnes, I used to do weight training with him. Later, when he moved to the Isle of Man I used to spend weekends with him and we would talk rugby among other things. I know he was proud when I became Great Britain captain and it was certainly a fantastic experience getting sound advice from one of the legendary figures in the game.

4. The great decline

"He is good in every department and a key man for Saints. There's always a cowboy trying to warm his lugs, but this doesn't put Harry off and he's always in the thick of things, starting attacks and destroying the opposition with some perfectly-measured defence-splitting passes."
Steve 'Knocker' Norton

It really did seem like the end of the good times at Knowsley Road as the new decade kicked in. Basically, the 1979–80 campaign was the worst suffered by the club for a long time. Looking at the statistics, we played 40 matches and lost 18 of them. Our league position was the worst for many years, eighth out of 16 teams, and we failed to make much of an impression in the cup competitions. It is true to say that the former 'Dad's Army' team of the mid-1970s was now well and truly in the throes of breaking up and we needed new blood in the team desperately. Young players were being drafted in, but they needed time to become established. There was one big signing pre-season, when Welsh international rugby union full-back Clive Griffiths joined us for a £25,000 fee. It was always going to be difficult for Clive to follow in the footsteps of players like Geoff Pimblett – another union signing – but he wanted to learn and play in our first match, against Widnes in the Lancashire Cup first round at Knowsley Road. We lost 28–16 – they also knocked us out of the John Player Trophy – but there were problems for Clive when he broke his arm in our second match, against Warrington at home in the league and Brian Parkes came in at full-back.

The transition wasn't easy for Clive, especially with the team struggling at times. His injury meant that I took over the goalkicking role and put 72 over in the season. But it was another responsibility that I could maybe have done without.

The squad was quite stable, really. As I said, Brian Parkes stepped into the full-back role. Les Jones occupied the right wing berth, with Roy Mathias on the left. Roy was still a powerful player and scored 27 tries that season, the same as another great footballer, Peter Glynn, who played at stand-off most of the time. Roy scored five tries and Glynn got a hat-trick against Workington just before Christmas; we won 51–0. Steve Peters and Derek Noonan were the centres. Two youngsters, Chris Arkwright and Roy Haggerty, made a huge impression. Neil Holding was first-choice scrum-half and the front row of the pack read Mel James (33 appearances), Graham Liptrot (36) and Eric Chisnall (33). It's well-known that Eric didn't relish playing in the front-row, but George Nicholls remained a stalwart in the second row and the club splashed out to sign Peter Gorley from Workington – a fantastic player of the Cumbrian granite variety. I remember he scored a try in his first game against Rochdale Hornets in the Floodlit Trophy at Knowsley Road and won the crowd over straight away. We scored eight tries and I kicked nine goals, from nine attempts – happy days.

From that game, we perked up and had a seven game unbeaten run, although we ended up losing 10–7 away to Hull KR in the Floodlit Trophy semi-final. That was the score at half-time. Not a point was scored after the interval. We did kick on afterwards and enjoyed some form in the league, including a 16–10 win against Wigan at Central Park. We won and I scored a hat-trick of tries. They certainly had a worse season than us, finishing fourth from bottom, with 21 points, five adrift from Workington Town above them. It meant relegation for the Cherry and Whites and although our spekkies were delighted, matches without Wigan on Boxing Day and Good Friday wouldn't quite be the same for the near future. The crowd that day was just over 7,000.

Unfortunately, just when we thought we were getting on a bit of a roll, Bradford Northern beat us by a single point at Knowsley Road, 11–10, in the second round of the Challenge Cup. We had 8,000 watching us and, quite understandably, there was disappointment among the fans when our road to Wembley ended. Results were patchy after that, to say the least and we won just four of our last 11 games. The last match of the season was away to Bradford Northern and they beat us 30–0.

I missed the last four matches through injury, having damaged knee ligaments in our 16–9 defeat at Naughton Park against Widnes, but I was feeling disappointed, overall, at the way things had gone. Injuries had taken their toll during the season, especially at the end and Eric Ashton could hardly name 15 players for the last game at Odsal.

For Lancashire, England and Great Britain

Although the 1979–80 season was quite disappointing for us as a team, the representative season was both busy and memorable for me and several of my team-mates. Lancashire won the County Championship and I made the transition from Under-24s rugby to the full England team. We topped the European Championship table, contested with France and Wales. I took part in six representative games during the season. I wonder what they would say about that today?

Although there was a poor crowd, it was still a great experience to play for Lancashire on my home turf of Knowsley Road against Cumbria. Chris Arkwright, who was making his county debut, scored a try and I kicked a drop-goal as we won fairly comfortably 23–15. But it was so disappointing to see such a low turn-out by the fans, 1,500, who missed a really good game.

St Helens RFC 1979–80: Back: Eric Ashton (coach), Chris Arkwright, Dave Chisnall, Keiron Pickavance, John Knighton, Mel James, Tom Ashcroft (chairman), Peter Gorley, Derek Noonan, Graham Liptrot, Harry Pinner, Eric Chisnall, Ken Henthorne (physio); front: Roy Mathias, Denis Litherland, Johnny Smith, Steve Peters, Neil Holding, George Nicholls (captain), Les Jones, Brian Parkes, Roy Haggerty, Peter Glynn, Clive Griffiths.

Our second game against Yorkshire at Castleford was lost by just three points, 19–16. I scored two tries in probably my best performance for the Red Rose County. This was all in the first half and I had to go off injured at half-time after I got concussed making a tackle. All three teams won a match and we topped the table as leading points scorers.

The Under-24 internationals against the French were always hard games for whatever reasons. For our first game at Leigh, with a French referee, we scored two tries from our wingers, Drummond and Fenton and were worthy winners, 14–2. I really looked forward to the return fixture, because it was my first game as captain of the Under-24s. Leigh's John Woods, the usual skipper, was injured.

We trained in the snow the day before in Carcassonne and I was confident, although I knew exactly what to expect. We knew that when we travelled over there it is going to be much harder, although Fred Lindop was an experienced referee who kept the lid on things as best he could. Our back three that day included a certain Kevin Ward, who had been showing up well in the league for his club, Castleford. But it was a real battle right from the start. Roy Holdstock flattened one of their centres and then our own centre, Mike Smith was poleaxed by a guy called Vidal. There was a big bust up after that with everything going in – boots, fists - the lot. Roy then got a flying kick in the throat that started the big fight. Lindop sent off Vidal and our Keith Rayne. So what did the new captain think of it all? Alan Thomas quoted me as follows: "We were on a hiding to nothing. We pulled it off for coach Whiteley. I did my best and so did all the lads. They were fantastic." I could have said a lot more,

35

but I think the press reports made it quite clear what we had to put up with! We came away battered and bruised, but at least we won 11–7. What a game it was for my team-mate Neil Holding to endure on his Under 24s debut as well. This is the Great Britain team that played in Carcassonne: Burke (Widnes 1G), Drummond (Leigh 1T), Stephenson (Salford 1T), Smith (Hull KR), Fenton (Castleford 1T), Rudd (Workington Town) Holding (St Helens), Holdstock (Hull KR), O'Neill (Salford), Keith Rayne (Wakefield Trinity), Ward (Castleford), James (Bramley), Pinner (St Helens). Subs: Dennison (Hull), Rathbone (Leigh).

In late February, I made my full England debut, against Wales in Hull. It was like they say in State of Origin, mate against mate, because there was quite a Saints contingent involved. Neil Holding and Peter Gorley were also playing their first game for England, with Graham Liptrot in reserve. Wales included front-rower Mel James, Chris Seldon and Roy Mathias, who played loose forward. In fact, Roy had played loose when I had been injured on a few occasions, so was no stranger to the position. The England team was coached by Eric Ashton and managed by St Helens director Joe Seddon, so it felt comfortable for me. There were five players with Hull connections, so the crowd was quite a good one. The Welsh, as ever, were tough opponents, but we beat them comfortably by four tries to one. I also banged over a couple of drop-goals for good measure. The press reports were favourable afterwards. David Hodgkinson in the *Rugby Leaguer* said that "...for me there was only one Man of the Match...Harry Pinner. He was in superb form, slipping out perfect passes, running with style and rugged determination, carving out openings in a worried welsh defence". It was nice to read reviews like this, but Neil Holding also had a superb game against Wigan's Ness Flowers and Peter Gorley cut them up in style.

European Championship
England (13) 26 Wales (4) 9
Friday 29 February 1980
Craven Park, Hull.
England: Fairbairn (Wigan 1T 6G), Wright (Widnes), Joyner (Castleford 1T), Smith (Hull KR), Drummond (Leigh), Evans (Featherstone Rovers), Holding (St Helens), Holdstock (Hull KR 1T), David Ward (Leeds), Keith Rayne (Wakefield Trinity 1T), Casey (Hull KR), Peter Gorley (St Helens), Pinner (St Helens (2DG)) Subs: Woods (Leigh), Grayshon (Bradford)
Wales: Box (Featherstone Rovers), Prendiville (Hull), Walters (Hull), Francis (Oldham), Juliff (Wakefield Trinity (1T)), Woods (Hull 3G), Flowers (Wigan), James (St Helens), Parry (Blackpool Borough), Shaw (Widnes), Seldon (St Helens), Bevan (Warrington), Mathias (St Helens) Subs: Diamond (Wakefield Trinity), McJennett (Barrow)
Referee: R. Campbell (Widnes)
Attendance: 7,557

We then went to France knowing that we had to beat them to win the Championship. Our referee was Billy Thompson, who, as was the custom, flew over with us. Arriving at the French airport before the match, his passport mysteriously found its way to me. It was quite hilarious watching Billy trying to explain to the French customs officials who he was and the fact that he obviously had his passport when he set off.

It was a really tough game in front of a huge crowd in Narbonne, with the local band creating a typical French rugby atmosphere. Overall there were not too many scoring chances created. We won in the end courtesy of a try from Steve Evans in the first half and a drop-goal from Alan Redfearn that clinched the championship. The French crowd got really upset when Billy disallowed a try with just two minutes to go that would have won the match for them. I kept a report of the match and it isn't necessary to read much French to realise that he got a lot of stick from the local press.

End of an era

It was announced in early April 1980, that our coach, Eric Ashton, would be leaving the club. Eric had been there for six years and was a tremendous help to me when I was making a bid to be an established first team player. The board loved him, he led the club to 10 major finals and would be sadly missed. Eric had been involved at the highest level as a player, player-coach and coach for a quarter of a century and perhaps thought he needed a break from the pressures of top level rugby league.

Unfortunately, I tended to feel the same as Eric in that I thought it was time I had a change. By the end of the 1979–80 season I really was quite adamant that I needed to leave Saints. It came to a situation where if the club didn't put me on the transfer list, I was not prepared to play. Obviously it didn't help the situation at the club, who were looking for a new coach, but I was quite prepared to carry on training by myself in the close season and see what happened. Perhaps I just needed a break myself after a hard season at club and representative level. I definitely thought, at the age of 24, that a change would do me good.

On 1 June, Saints appointed Kel Coslett as the new coach. He had previously coached Rochdale Hornets and had been on a non-contract appointment at Wigan from October 1979 to April 1980.

George Fairbairn went on to become player-coach at Central Park. Kel was a Saints legend and a nice guy, but he had problems to solve straight away. I was in dispute; Eric Chisnall was also unsettled and there were rumours that Workington wanted to re-sign Peter Gorley at a record fee. Club secretary Geoff Sutcliffe, as usual, tried to do his best to defuse the situation by saying that Saints could not afford to let quality forwards go.

St Helens 10 Bradford Northern 21, 23 September 1979. George Nicholls, with the ball, is not happy with Bradford prop Colin Forsyth. Harry is at acting half-back. (Photo: Brian Peers)

Widnes 31 St Helens 20 (John Player Trophy), 30 September 1979. Harry showing that he could tackle. (Photo: Brian Peers)

So I trained by myself and still watched games at the start of the 1980–81 season. It was on a Friday evening, in late August that I gave Kel a ring and we met with chairman Tom Ashcroft to see what would happen.

They were very supportive of my return to training, although Kel did emphasise that I had to fight hard to get my place in the team back. He reckoned both parties had been losers; I had not been playing and the club had lost the services of an international forward. Anyhow, it was great to be welcomed back, although I did think that there would be more problems ahead for us as team building continued. It wouldn't be easy to restore our reputation as a top club once more, certainly not in the short term. In my absence, George Nicholls played in the number 13 jersey. He left for Cardiff Blue Dragons at the end of the season after a well-deserved testimonial at Knowsley Road.

In many ways, the 1980–81 season was very much like the previous one, as we finished in eighth place in the league, winning half our games and drawing one for a total of 31 points. Bradford Northern, with their big pack of forwards were back-to-back champions with 41 points. Ironically, one of our best performances came right at the end of the season, when we went to Odsal and turned them over 14–12. Yet we lost to Hull KR in the Premiership semi-final at Craven Park. We were knocked out of the Lancashire Cup – by Widnes – and the John Player Trophy – by Warrington – in the first round. However, we did well in the Challenge Cup, reaching the semi-final, where we played Hull KR at Headingley. Rovers were a solid team and beat us 22–5, but were themselves defeated at Wembley by Widnes.

As for new faces in the Saints' team, Chris Arkwright was now fully established at centre and Mike Hope had impressed in the number 10 jersey. There was another new signing in the front row: Roger Owen, from Llanelli Dock Stars. He hadn't got a full cap for Wales in union like Clive Griffiths, but still received a hefty fee to change codes. Roger played 13 matches that season, with our spekkies wondering whether he had what it took to make the grade. My early absence from the Saints' team had a knock-on effect with loose-forward Mick Adams selected for Lancashire in the County Championship, which was won by the Cumbrians.

At club level, one of our most satisfying performances at Knowsley Road was the defeat of the visiting Kiwis. We won 11–6. I thought I had played well and might have caught the eye of the selectors for the test matches. Just for the record, the Saints' team that downed the mighty Kiwis was: Griffiths (4G), Jones (1T), Litherland, Haggerty, Mathias, Parkes, Holding, James, Nulty, Hope, Eric Chisnall, Nicholls, Pinner. Subs: Smith and Pickavance. Take a bow, lads.

St Helens 11 New Zealand 6, 12 October 1980.
Harry has just put front-rower Mike Hope into the gap. A memorable win
against the Kiwis. (Photo: Brian Peers)

I was delighted to be selected on the bench for the first test against the
Kiwis at Central Park. This was after nine matches with the Under-24s; I
thought I was worthy of the step up. Len Casey of Hull KR was in the
number 13 jersey and I was the only St Helens player in the team.

There were five players from Hull KR in the first XIII, which showed
their strength at the time. Seven players, including me, were making our
full test match debuts for Great Britain: Chris Camilleri, Keith Bentley,
Steve Hartley, Kevin Dick, Roy Holdstock and Les Gorley. Fairbairn was
captain for the first time. In the end, both teams scored two tries and
four goals and the match was drawn. I came on for Trevor Skerrett and
was involved in the move that saw Mike Smith go in under the posts to
give us the lead in the second half. Gordon Smith's penalty four minutes
from time levelled the scores, although Fairbairn had an attempt at a 50
yard penalty on the final hooter that went just wide. The critics said we
were lucky to get a draw, but we didn't really care. They were a tough
side and tried to assert their authority with a big brawl after the first
scrum. I was glad to be on the subs' bench for that one.

Test Match No. 211
Great Britain (9) 14 New Zealand (10) 14
Saturday 18 October 1980
Central Park, Wigan
Great Britain: Fairbairn (Wigan Capt. 4G), Camilleri (Barrow 1T), Joyner
(Castleford), Mike Smith (Hull KR 1T), Bentley (Widnes), Hartley (Hull KR), Dick
(Leeds), Holdstock (Hull KR), Watkinson (Hull KR), Skerrett (Hull), Grayshon

(Bradford Northern), Les Gorley (Widnes), Casey (Hull KR). Subs: Pinner (St Helens), Burke (Widnes)
New Zealand: O'Donnell, Fisher, Dickison, Leuluai, O'Hara, Ah Kuoi (1T), Gordon Smith (4G), Broadhurst, Rushton, Tamati, West, Coll (1T), Graham. Subs: Baxendale, Whittaker
Referee: W. Thompson (Huddersfield)
Attendance: 7,031

The selectors made a few changes for the second test at Odsal. I came into the line-up at loose forward and Des Drummond came in on the right wing for his Great Britain debut, with Glyn Shaw replacing Skerrett also for his first match at test level. It was, apparently, the last test match staged at Odsal, but we didn't give the fans much to shout about. The score flattered us, as New Zealand were the better side by far. Dane O'Hara's try after 67 minutes sealed the victory for them, but everyone knew they were worthy winners. It wasn't really my day and I had to be substituted at half-time with a sprung shoulder, after I tackled their right centre, Whittaker, who was a really strong runner.

I had found it difficult to get into the game and dominate. Having said that, we made too many errors and their first try, when their full-back, Michael O'Donnell, went in at the corner after selling an outrageous dummy, should have been prevented.

Test Match No. 212
Great Britain (6) 8 New Zealand (9) 12
Sunday 2 November 1980
Odsal Stadium, Bradford
Great Britain: Fairbairn (Wigan Capt 4G), Drummond (Leigh), Joyner (Castleford), Smith (Hull KR), Camilleri (Barrow), Kelly (Warrington), Dick (Leeds), Holdstock (Hull KR), Elwell (Widnes), Shaw (Widnes), Grayshon (Bradford Northern), Casey (Hull KR), Pinner (St Helens) Subs: Evans (Featherstone Rovers), Les Gorley (Widnes).
New Zealand: O'Donnell (1T), Prohm, Whittaker, Leuluai, O'Hara (1T), Ah Kuoi, Gordon Smith (3G), Broadhurst, Rushton, Tamati, West, Coll, Graham. Subs: Baxendale, Fisher.
Referee: Fred Lindop (Wakefield)
Attendance: 10,946.

I didn't play in the final test, at Headingley, but in wet and very greasy conditions, Great Britain levelled the series with a 10–2 victory. Peter Gorley made his full Great Britain debut in the match, so I was naturally pleased for him, though disappointed that I was not involved. It was certainly an experience sampling rugby at that level and I certainly came across several of the New Zealand lads when they played for British clubs afterwards, such as Gary Prohm, Gordon Smith and Mark Broadhurst at

41

Hull KR; James Leuluai, Dane O'Hara and Fred Ah Kuoi at Hull, Kevin Tamati at Warrington and Graham West at Wigan.

1981–82: The season from hell

Representative rugby league was proving to be a welcome, if incredibly tough distraction from life at Knowsley Road. We had signed John Butler at the start of the 1981–82 season and followed it up in November 1981 with Gary Moorby, from Keighley, who was a 'strike' forward, to partner Peter Gorley in the second row. This was a real gamble, as Gary cost the club a £37,000 fee. Overall, we lacked strength in depth and were over-powered in many games. Injuries to Neil Holding, who had to have a shoulder-pinning operation at the start of the season and, later, Graham Liptrot with a broken jaw, did our cause no good at all. I struggled with a hamstring injury that I found hard to shrug off. I made my come-back from the bench against Widnes on New Year's Day, which turned out to be a bit of a farce for the fans. The pitch was shrouded in fog and most people couldn't really see much, especially those in the Main Stand.

The referee, Stan Wall, had to keep time himself because he couldn't signal to the timekeepers in the stand. He applied the rules before the match in that he had to stand on the centre spot and see the corner flags, so he had no option but to call the game on. Incredibly, it was Saints' first home match for 11 weeks, since our drawn Lancashire Cup tie with Barrow on 18 October. Supporters only knew who scored in the first half after an announcement by Geoff Sutcliffe on the public address.

Our next game was at Headingley, where we were beaten by a Leeds team struggling for form themselves 30–4. This was the beginning of seven defeats in 10 matches including a 20–12 defeat at the hands of the old enemy, Wigan, in the Challenge Cup first round at Knowsley Road. I didn't think they were a particularly good side, but they were coached by Maurice Bamford, who later was my coach with the Great Britain team in 1985. 'Lippy' dominated the scrums, but we had a 'good' try from Gary Moorby disallowed and things went from bad to worse. Our front row that day was Allan Rowley, on loan from Barrow, Lippy and Roger Owen. Eric Chisnall and Gary Moorby were also in the back row, with me at 13. For the next game at York, a rare win – 19–7 – Eric was in the front-row; Colin Whittle at hooker and Roger Owen at 10.

We also ended the season badly, with four defeats from seven. Hull KR ended any lingering hopes we had of finishing in the top four with a 28–16 win at Knowsley Road – their first for over half a century. We did make a good fist of it, but were over-powered. We really did miss 'Lippy' in the scrums and I still didn't feel as though I was firing on all cylinders.

Warrington 13 St. Helens 11, 4 October 1981.
Saints line up at Wilderspool: Back: Roger Owen (Sub), Roy Haggerty, Harry Pinner, Peter Glynn, Peter Gorley, Roy Mathias, Mike Hope, Denis Litherland (Sub); front: Graham Liptrot, Brian Parkes, Steve Peters, Eric Chisnall (Capt), Johnny Butler, Kevin Meadows, Mel James. (Courtesy Alex Service)

But one game, in particular, really upset the supporters, when we lost to Castleford at home on 20 January 1982. I was still struggling to regain full fitness and watched as the visitors were 31–0 up at half-time and their front – rower, Barry Johnson, a team-mate of mine from the Great Britain Under-24s, just cut us to pieces. Things weren't as bad after half-time and the final score was 40–10, but it triggered off much bad feeling, shown by several letters in the local press. "Sorry, Saints ... you've had the last of my support and my money," wrote one irate spekkie.

I have to say they had a point and, of course, it was upsetting for all of us. What it would be like today with social media I shudder to think. There were 3,338 fans there for the game and a major reason why the club was so desperately short of money. In the end, we were all called in to a 'showdown' meeting with the board.

We had conceded 97 points in the last three matches, so this course of action was hardly surprising. It was clearly not a time to show too much panic and Kel remained in charge, which was perhaps a wise thing for them to do. But there was only so much he could do with the players at his disposal and the injury situation in particular. It is interesting to compare it with the 2014 season at Saints when chairman Eamonn McManus gave his team a 'pep' talk, but they were in a much better position than we were at the time and went on win the Grand Final.

43

St Helens 16 Hull KR 28, 4 April 1982.
'Follow me boys, and I'll put you through.' Gary Moorby (nearest left) and
Denis Litherland are willing runners. (Photo: Brian Peers)

Memories are short in circumstances like these, but we had produced some brilliant rugby earlier on in the season and beat Castleford 32–17 at Wheldon Road. Just to show how good that victory was, Castleford won the penalty count 15–7, but Graham Liptrot dominated the scrums as he usually did, 9–4. Welsh centre Steve Bayliss got a hat-trick. He was a straight-running and powerful player, who was difficult to stop on his way to the line. I thought I was back to my best form after I asked to be put on the transfer list at the start of the season. I was listed at £80,000. I then wrote to the club asking to be taken off it and then, lo and behold, Wigan came in for me with a £70,000 offer. It was 24 hours before their AGM and they obviously wanted another 'marquee' signing to please the fans. After all, they had got out of the Second Division at the first attempt and were keen to reinforce their team on their return to the top flight. They were getting good crowds and had plenty of cash to splash about. Saints secretary Geoff Sutcliffe put out a 'hands off' and 'Harry is not for sale' piece in the press to put the club's viewpoint forward. He went on to say: "There is a lot of potential about the team now and there's no way we want to lose a player of Harry's ability." If only he knew how the season would eventually unfold.

The break-up of the 'old guard' continued when Eric Chisnall, who was always unhappy at being selected in the front row, was transferred to Leigh for £15,000. He had been at Saints since the 1966–67 season and was joining a club, under Alex Murphy, which would end up as champions. Apparently he was on the verge of quitting altogether after a series of disagreements with Kel Coslett. His last game was the Wigan cup tie and it was not the sort of finale he wanted for his last match at Saints after such a long career.

As it happened, I took over the captaincy, which was always a particular ambition of mine, although the need to win games was always on my mind after the disastrous mid-season slump.

Perhaps we knew it was coming, but it was still a shock when the club announced that Kel would not be retained as first team coach. According to the local press Kel felt as though he had been 'stabbed in the back' by the board. He had always wanted to coach the club and we all had a great deal of sympathy for him and what he had done. He outlined: "I said two years ago there was a lot of work to be done and it would take time. The camp was split, there was a lot of trouble and discontent. All that is now gone. There is a tremendous spirit within the side. I feel let down by the board. I have been thrown out when all the hard work has been done... the teams who finished above us in the league are teams who have gone out and bought big name players. We can't afford to do that. Our way forward is through the youth policy."

Injuries had always been a problem over the past two years, as I can testify. In terms of team-building, perhaps there was too much emphasis on signings from the other code, rather than buying existing stars from other clubs. A few weeks before the Wigan cup tie there had been talk of the club making overtures to England rugby union wingers Mike Slemen and John Carleton. Earlier in the year, Saints were also linked with Henderson Gill and thought the price too expensive. He later joined Wigan and would have been a sensation at Knowsley Road. He ended up knocking us out of the Challenge Cup with one of his tries.

By the middle of May, 1982, while Saints had the coaching problem to solve, it was reported in the press that Wigan once again wanted me to play for them. "Hands off Pinner" was the headline in the *St Helens Reporter,* again. Geoff Sutcliffe was quoted as saying: "There is no way we will be letting Pinner leave Knowsley Road. He is the cornerstone of our team. It's a team we want to build around him."

Wigan had also just sacked Maurice Bamford as coach and were looking for a successor, but in the end, it was unlikely I would leave Saints for Central Park, even though I had been on the list earlier in the season. I was the team captain and quite settled and the club would only sell me for probably a record sum. "Wigan would have to sell half of Central Park to raise enough money for Pinner," said Geoff in another article – an interesting thought, but I suppose it was nice to feel wanted! And surely we couldn't have another season like the last one at Knowsley Road. I convinced myself that we were on an upward curve and there were much better times around the corner.

In Saints' new jerseys, early in 1983–84 – a change from the traditional
red vee. (Photo: Brian Peers)

5. Stirring the sleeping giant

"Harry has something of a Midas touch on the field. Like the ancient king, everything he touches appears to turn to gold. Harry is not a great conversationalist off the field. He likes to keep himself to himself. However, it is a different story on the field – there he likes to dictate events and lead Saints superbly as skipper."
Steve Nicholson

The 1982–83 season saw the Saints team still largely in a period of transition and rebuilding. We had a change of coach, with Billy Benyon brought in to replace Kel Coslett. Now, I had a good relationship with Kel, one of mutual respect and, of course, he had been the captain when I first broke in to the first team in 1975–76. But I think the board thought that a change was what was needed. I believe the club approached Alex Murphy first of all, but he turned them down and signed a four-year contract at Leigh.

At the end of May, I was delighted to learn that the club had decided to go for Billy Benyon, who was another Saints' 'great' as a player. He was a real legend, who had come up through the junior ranks, and went on to play over 500 games for the club. Personally, I had a huge respect for Billy as a player. He was a team-mate of mine when he was in the veteran stage, but always came across as a brilliant professional. As a coach he was certainly a good appointment as far as I was concerned. He knew the players and it was the start of a fantastic relationship. I would have run through a brick wall for him, as would all the other lads. Billy had done well in his first few seasons as coach at Warrington, initially taking over from Alex Murphy in 1978, who had left Wilderspool for Salford. Unfortunately, results had not gone Billy's way after several years of success and he was dismissed in March 1982. Just after he joined us at Saints he was involved in a successful wrongful dismissal case. Their loss was definitely our gain, in my opinion.

On a personal note it was another ambition fulfilled for me when I was appointed club captain and 1982–83 would be my first full season in the job. As a local lad, who always wanted to play for the Saints, to become captain was a dream come true and a great source of pride. Don't get me wrong, I was never necessarily over-awed by the prospect of leading the team. I had played with the famous Dad's Army team of the 1970s and picked up so much experience of taking part in big matches. That team had virtually all gone now and I was proud to take the captaincy over from Eric Chisnall, who had gone to Leigh. In fact, perhaps only Roy Mathias and arguably Mel James were still around from the 'glory years'.

It was time for a change and there was a new team to develop. We had to put recent past glories to one side and concentrate on the present and although the team was very much in the developing stage, there were a number of young, local lads breaking through who really could make their mark. We just needed a bit of time. I was perhaps in my pomp age-wise and felt that I could do a really good job, but at the same time I realised that it wasn't going to be easy.

Being captain meant other responsibilities off the field as well, which I didn't think would be a problem, including my article for the Supporters Club Handbook for the new season, 1982–83. This was what I wrote: "Season 1981–82 may not have been one to remember for the average Saints' supporters based on success over the years. It will be remembered within the club for the alarming crop of injuries which dogged almost all the players at sometimes during the season. Out of this though came the encouraging signs for our younger players thrown in at the deep end, and in some cases, playing in unaccustomed positions, and they came out of it with valuable experience. This must surely stand the club in good stead for the seasons to come."

I thought it was fair comment and that our situation would improve if we could only get a settled side together. We had what I thought was a good attacking 'spine' in the team, with my prompting out wide, probing for gaps bringing lads onto the ball; there was Graham Liptrot, one of the greatest hookers ever, who would dominate scrum possession in most games, patrol the play-the-ball area and give us a marvellous attacking dimension. There was the fantastic pace of scrum-half Neil Holding. This lad really did have pace to burn and frightened opposing defenders to death. But we mustn't forget that he was also a good play-maker in his own right with good vision and handling skills. If we remained largely injury-free, I was sure that this attacking unit would come up with the goods, but, of course, there was more to it than that.

Incidentally going back to that same handbook, the chairman, Tom Ashcroft – John Clegg took over shortly after when his three year term was up – talked about the money side in his pre-season message to the fans. It was obvious that the club was not well-off financially and had just recorded a loss on the previous season of over £50,000. Tom made reference to this and reading between the lines, the supporters felt that there was not much chance of major big signings coming to St Helens. Those in the squad would just have to roll up their sleeves and have a go. He wrote: "Unfortunately, the financial side of our game is becoming increasingly difficult and we have no magic wand to bring about a solution. The only way forward and up is by enthusiasm and sheer hard grafting at every level throughout the club."

To be fair, his hands were tied because our gates, the major form of revenue in those days, were not good and we averaged 4,543 for the season – not like the modern Saints, when attendances at the new stadium at Langtree Park are mostly on or near the five figure mark. In fact the whole country was in recession in the early 1980s and money was tight. Clubs did a lot of loan deals, as they simply did not have the cash. Looking through one of the old programmes for the time is interesting, as it shows a great big list of those players on the transfer list at Knowsley Road in November 1982 and they had, in most cases, had their possible transfer fees reduced by the Board: Les Jones £2,000 (£5,000); Steve Bayliss £40,000 (£45,000); Tony Bolton £3,000 (£4,000); Paul Brownbill £4,000 (£6,000); David Fairclough £3,000 (£5,000); Peter Glynn £25,000 (£30,000); Mike Hope £5,000 (£8,000); Garry Irvine £1,000 (£2,000); Denis Nulty £3,000 (£6,000); Roger Owen £15,000 (£20,000); Steve Peters £40,000 (£60,000). Unchanged: Brian Parkes £15,000; Johnny Smith £6,000; Added to list: Clive Griffiths £12,000

The one 'success' in the market was Steve Bayliss, who brought in £40,000 when he eventually moved to Fulham, but the message was clear – the club had to sell to buy and the market was virtually flat. It was going to be the year of the underdog in some ways, but that now included ourselves. The boom area of the game was in Humberside, where Hull and Hull KR were very difficult to beat and favourites for most of the major honours.

Tough and tougher

These days Super League teams plan their pre-season by easing their squads into action with a series of 'warm-up' friendlies before the main competition starts. We didn't do that at the start of the 1982–83 season. We started with the 'friendly' with Pilkington Recs at Knowsley Road, which was a testimonial match for Roy Mathias. It seemed a good idea, I suppose, as the Recs had been a professional team years ago and there was a bit of rivalry at that time in the town. Although we beat the modern-day amateur Recs quite comfortably, it was certainly a fierce contest, with Roy and the Recs' Kevin Whittle having a right set-to at one stage. Some friendly. Then we played Oldham, again at home – Andy Platt's debut – where we didn't play well and Billy gave us a right dressing-down afterwards.

The season started with a visit to Leigh, who were league champions. We did really well to hold them to a 19–19 draw. Neil Holding kicked a last-minute conversion from the touchline after Gary Bottell's try right on the hooter. Their fans thought that it was no try and gave referee John McDonald loads of stick. But it was an encouraging start and we followed it up with a win against Bradford Northern at Knowsley Road. This was another thriller.

St Helens 10
Leigh 19,
10 October
1982
Running at
Tommy
Martyn and
the Leigh
defence.
(Courtesy
Brian Peers)

St Helens RFC 1982–83: Back: Chris Arkwright, Paul Round, Mike Hope, Gary
Moorby, Paul Brownbill, Brian Gelling, Mick Glover, Peter Glynn, Roy Mathias,
Roy Haggerty; middle: Kevin Wellens, Andy Platt, Barry Ledger, Gary Bottell,
Tony Bolton, Denis Litherland, Mel James, Graham Liptrot, Billy Benyon
(coach), Eric Leach (kitman); front: Neil Holding, Steve Peters, Colin Whittle,
Tom Ashcroft (vice chairman), Harry Pinner (captain), John Clegg (chairman),
Johnny Smith, Kevin Meadows, Johnny Butler.
(Courtesy Alex Service)

50

St Helens 10 Featherstone Rovers 11 (Challenge Cup), 12 March 1983.
Saints' Wembley hopes went up in smoke. Chris Arkwright is held by some
determined Featherstone Rovers defenders. David Hobbs (right) has just
tackled Harry and doesn't want to let go. Saints lost and the fans were, quite
naturally, a bit fed up. (Courtesy Brian Peers)

Celebrating Saints' sponsorship with McEwan Youngers, with Billy Benyon
and John Clegg. (Courtesy Harry Pinner)

We won 12–11 and I managed to get the winning drop-goal two minutes from time, although their stand-off Dean Carroll had a go later on and hit the post. This was when I was starting to get a reputation as a drop-goal expert. I used to practise this type of kick in the early days when my dad used to help me out. He helped me by throwing the ball to the opposite side than I had kicked it from and in doing so, it improved my confidence to have a go from either side of the posts, but always with my left foot. The next match brought us down to earth at Hull KR. They really gave me – or anyone else for that matter – no space to work in at all and there were always three defenders waiting to try and blot out anything creative from us.

Perhaps one of our best chances of success was in the Lancashire Cup. We won at Widnes and were the first team to knock Widnes out in the First round since 1973. We went to Barrow where we won 9–6 in the second round. We played them again straight after in the league and lost 19–12. Roy Haggerty got sent off as well. There was a flare up following on from an incident in the first game when he – allegedly – broke Steve Herbert's nose. I do remember when play resumed, sending in young Andy Platt for a try, but it was all in vain. New club Carlisle came to Knowsley Road in the semi-final and we drew 7–7. I remember missing a few chances to win the game with drop-goal attempts that went hopelessly wide and, fortunately, full-back Jimmy Birts did the same for Carlisle. We ended up getting through to the final with a 9–5 victory in the replay at Carlisle United's Brunton Park. Lippy won the scrums 11–4; Denis Litherland scored our try and I kicked three drop-goals, with Neil Holding banging over another drop-goal and conversion. We enjoyed the well-earned celebrations in the dressing room later.

Billy Benyon was really buzzing, especially when we knew it would be Warrington in the final. In one newspaper he said how badly he wanted to win the Lancashire Cup and how it would set the ball rolling for a new era of success for the club. It was our first county cup final appearance for 12 years and although it was still a good achievement to get there, especially beating Widnes, the next few weeks would see the St Helens club fall out with the fans and generally commit public relations suicide.

From bad to worse

It should have been one of the show-piece games of the season at Knowsley Road when the Australian tourists came. As it was, the team had a number of cry-offs because the Lancashire Cup final was seven days away. I was carrying a couple of knocks and they wouldn't risk me in such a game, but there were others, like Roy Haggerty, Gary Bottell, Johnny Butler and Graham Liptrot who were not included. In the end we played an important game with a severely weakened team in front of our biggest crowd of the season and were blown away by a side which went through the tour unbeaten. There were over 8,000 people there, only the gate against Wigan was bigger, and they saw a 'different class' Australian side over-power us. In fact it was almost a full test side: Brentnall, Boustead, Meninga, Rogers, Grothe, Kenny, Sterling, Young, Krilich, Boyd, Pearce, Muggleton, Price, with Morris and my favourite Australian player, Wally Lewis, on the bench.

The Australians were not too pleased about our team selection and there was a real stink about it in the media. One newspaper headline said it all: 'Big Crowd see Big Non-Event!' Geoff Sutcliffe was also very honest about the whole thing: "I feel very sorry for the fans and everyone involved with the club. It was an embarrassment and if I had paid to see the game I would have felt very angry!" It was exhibition stuff from the Aussies and the result, 32–0, meant that Saints might not be considered for a tourist game when the Kangaroos came over in 1986.

As for the final against Warrington we went into it looking to win, but things just didn't seem to go our way. We couldn't argue with the result on paper. We ended up with the big fat zero. Warrington scored 16. We were all a bit fed up, as were the supporters. In our defence, although we didn't seem to have much on the day, we played quite well in the first half, but couldn't score. Their first try was when Hesford caught his own 'bomb' and put his winger, Fellows, over. We folded a bit after half-time and 'Lippy' was sent off for a late tackle on his opposite number Carl Webb. As usual, he was dominating the scrums 3–1 at the time. Their back-rowers ground us down after that and we were never in with a shout.

Lancashire Cup Final
St Helens (0) 0 Warrington (3) 16
Saturday 23 October 1982
Central Park, Wigan
St Helens: Parkes, Ledger, Arkwright, Haggerty, Litherland; Peters, Holding, James, Liptrot, Bottell, Moorby, Gorley, Pinner (Capt)
Subs: Smith (for Parkes), Mathias (for Bottell)
Warrington: Hesford (2G), Fellows (1T), Duane, Bevan, Mike Kelly (1T), Cullen, Ken Kelly (Capt 1T), Courtney, Webb, Cooke, Eccles (1T), Fieldhouse, Gregory
Subs: Finnigan, Chisnall (for Cooke)
Referee: J. Holdsworth (Leeds)
Attendance: 6,462

Billy Benyon was furious with our performance. The stuff he gave the reporters afterwards wasn't quite as colourful as what he said to us: "They all wanted winners' medals, but how a team with so many experienced players, internationals around them, can offer hardly a threat after winning the scrums 14–4 is beyond me. It's upsetting. I thought our preparation was right but we just aren't good enough. I'm confident I can do my job but not overnight. I need help!"

Calm down Billy. I presume he wanted some new signings, rather than a doctor, preferably forwards like Brian Case and Ian Potter, both local lads, but with the financial situation, it seemed unlikely. Things were not going too well at Knowsley Road and obviously as captain, I was getting quite a bit of stick from the spekkies. The club had to do something to improve the situation and shortly afterwards announced that they had signed the big front-rower Paul Grimes from Whitehaven. Although he was a Geordie by birth, I think a move to Saints suited him because his wife was a local girl, from Haydock, and a big Saints fan. He was experienced and had played for Leigh at Wembley, but the thing about him was the way he lined players up in the tackle and hit them hard with his shoulder. He wouldn't be allowed to do that today.

Paul never took a backward step and was a good signing for us, maybe not the superstar the fans might have wanted, but he gave us added strength in the pack. Funnily enough, the Brian Case thing wouldn't go away and at one stage, Warrington wanted to swap him for Steve Peters, who was on the transfer list at the time for £60,000. Case went to Wigan in the end, in a straight cash deal. He would have been a good signing for us, but it wasn't to be.

Onwards and upwards?

Ironically, our next match was at home to Warrington. We had a front-row of Grimes and Mel James, both well in their 30s and won 16–11 with tries from Roy Haggerty, Roy Mathias and a lad who I thought was a much under-rated player, Peter Glynn. He could play at centre or stand-off, had great finishing ability, pace and good hands. It was a mystery to me why he was allowed to go to Salford at the end of the season. So at least we had pleased the crowd, not that there were that many at the game: 4,611.

I loved one of the comments in the press afterwards: "Saints showed a refreshing urgency to pocket winning pay." Too right we did. We started to play with renewed confidence for a spell and I remember when we played Fulham in the first round of the John Player Trophy, the club was featured in a BBC documentary when we were compared with Sale Rugby Union Club. They showed how we trained, some clips from match action – Peter Glynn scored another superb try for us that day – and stuff from behind the scenes. Both clubs needed money to keep going, but there was much made of the fact that the Sale lads 'paid to play' with their subs; we obviously looked forward to our pay packets, but the thing that didn't come across was the fact that we were not just money-grabbing mercenaries. We enjoyed playing and had our own social side as well. In the end was the usual argument as to who would win if the teams played each other. Ray French said we would win easily, but little did anyone realise that 20 years later the two teams, then both fully-professional, would play each other in a friendly at Knowsley Road – half union, half league. I think Apollo Perelini was involved with this at some point. It just showed that union was far more technical and how different the two games were.

We lost 9–5 to Wigan in the next round of the John Player Trophy at Central Park, once again despite Lippy dominating Nicky Kiss 16–11 in the scrums. The penalty count, 18–11 to Wigan, probably cost us the match in the end. We then hit a real purple patch from late December to early March, when we made a real bid for a top four place in the First Division table with eight wins from nine matches. We made progress in the Challenge Cup as well, probably our most realistic chance for honours. Carlisle came first and we beat them 52–0, although they were in financial trouble and had lost a number of the players who gave us trouble in the Lancashire Cup ties. It seemed difficult to go to Headingley and beat Leeds in the next round, but we did. We won 23–13 and it was our 10th win in 11 outings. I had the time and space to have a hand in three of our four tries, but, once again, it was all down to 'Lippy' who dominated the scrums 18–4. Leeds's normal number nine, David Ward, a brilliant player, had been suspended and a lad called Russell Sowden took his place. It was no contest.

Just like with Warrington, the fixture list meant that Leeds came to Knowsley Road after the cup tie and we beat them again, 19–7. The team seemed to be playing with great confidence and we drew Featherstone Rovers at home in the quarter-finals, a team who had inflicted defeat on Saints in the past, but on current form, we were clear favourites, having beaten them twice in the league matches.

It was a chance to show that our recent improvement was no fluke and to give the fans the chance of a Wembley visit. Unfortunately, things did not go our way once again, just when they needed to. I had a groin injury early on, which didn't help things, but we never seemed to get going and a lot of the lads struggled to make an impression. They won 11–10 and the try that beat us was scored by a long-haired lad called John Gilbert, after 71 minutes. Gary Moorby tried to play the ball to himself near the Featherstone line. He was penalised and they came down the field and scored. Their hooker, the veteran Ray Handscombe won some vital scrums for them early on, no mean feat against Lippy, and their forwards just seemed to get the better of us. Like all the lads, I was really upset. In the local paper I was quoted as saying: "Billy [Benyon] has got us ticking – now we've gone and let down everyone in town!"

As it happened, we did go out to the eventual winners of the competition, as Rovers went on to beat Hull in a classic final, but it was no consolation whatsoever. We lost a bit of momentum towards the end of the season and were beaten at Wigan 13–6 on Good Friday. Then Widnes beat us at Knowsley Road on Easter Monday. Out of the last nine games, we won four, although we just made the top four. I damaged my ankle and missed the last five games. The team lost at Widnes in the first round of the Premiership and poor old 'Lippy' went into a tackle on Widnes loose forward Mick Adams and reeled away.

He just walked to the dressing room. He knew what the damage was. It was his third broken jaw in just over two years, a real tragedy. I remember one time we visited him in hospital after having his jaw wired and he didn't appreciate our present to him. I can't think why – it was the best treacle toffee money could buy.

My ankle kept swelling up every time I played and there was a lump on it the size of a golf ball. I went to see an osteopath, who had me balance on a wobble-board to strengthen it. I also had my own personal trainer – Kenny Gill. I think that Saints had wanted to bring him out of retirement earlier on in the season, but he didn't want to resume playing. He told me I would be a better player if I was fitter. Now ... I always thought I was quite fit anyway, but went along with him and it did me the world of good. Kenny, who was landlord of the Derby Arms in Rainford at the time was certainly fit and really put me through the mill. We would do 200s and 400s sprints; road runs, fell-walking and bike riding. I certainly felt the benefit of what we did and felt that my own preparation for the new season, 1983–84, was spot on.

The team had done well, in the end, to reach the top four. Looking at the lads who played the most games during the season is interesting as well. Top of the list with 37 appearances and top try-scorer with 18 was Roy Haggerty. He was utterly fearless, a Saint through and through and probably, in the nicest sense, completely un-coachable, but a great character and real fans' favourite. Peter Gorley and Mel James played in 35 matches. Peter was strong and forceful and a good runner with the ball. Such a pity we could never get his brother Les over to Saints. They would have been as good a combination as anyone in that second row.

As for Mel, he had played his 300th game by the end of the season and was a 'bookend' prop who stood no nonsense. Young winger Barry Ledger played in 33 matches and was starting to show the form that would help him play for Great Britain, he was so fast and elusive. Scrum-half Neil Holding also played in the same number. Always a real bubbly character and so dangerous on the field with his pace, he also was the leading goalkicker with 47. Chris Arkwright, Gary Moorby and Lippy made 31 appearances. Arkie's best position for me was stand-off, rather than centre, but he played well wherever he was selected. He could pass a ball and was quite ferocious. I remember him having a right 'do' with a young Kiwi centre called Dean Bell, who was playing for Carlisle, in the Lancashire Cup semi-final. It didn't bother Chris who it was – he was another who would never step backwards. Gary Moorby was built like a modern-day Super League player, with good upper body strength and he was a capable running forward, scoring 13 tries. He scored four at home to Workington in the league, when they had to wear our change jerseys because of a colour clash. What can be said about 'Lippy'? He made winning the ball in the scrums look easy at times and it was so tragic when he broke his jaw for the third time. He would moan like hell at anyone if he wasn't getting the ball, which was rare. Neil Holding was first in line; then it was his front-rowers, then back-rows and ultimately me, I suppose.

My own tally was 30 matches, although at the end of the season, I became the first winner of the Slalom Lager/*Daily Star* Player of the Year Award, a nice trophy and £500 prize money, despite missing those last five games. Happy days. But I would have swapped all that for a Lancashire Cup winner's medal or a trip to Wembley, or, maybe a crack at the Australians in a Great Britain jersey.

A new start

I felt fitter than I had done for a long while after my workouts with Ken Gill and looked forward to the new season, 1983–84, with reasonable optimism. There was the usual speculation, or, as the spekkies used to call them: 'Irons in the fire', linking Saints with various transfer targets. These included Salford winger Keith Fielding, Barrow's full-back Steve Tickle, who was a St Helens lad and Dean Bell. I'm sure Arkie would have welcomed him with open arms. Roy Haggerty put in a transfer request and was on the list at £65,000, but wasn't really going anywhere. Billy Benyon signed a new 12 month contract, so that was good by me! We all hoped that the 'Sleeping Giants' that Saints had become would continue to rise from their slumber, but in the case of St Helens RFC at the time, no one could predict what would happen. We had the introduction of the four-point try, and something which would shape the game over the next few years – the ending of the six-year ban on transfers between Britain and Australia.

We began like a house on fire, beating Champions Hull KR 30–11 at Knowsley Road, including a superb 70 yard try from young winger Barry Ledger just before the hooter, which reminded the fans of Tom van Vollenhoven at his best. This was an important game for me, because Frank Myler, the Great Britain coach, was watching and gave me the Man-of-the-Match award. It was a good start for me to try and impress for an eventual tour place to Australia and New Zealand at the end of the season. The press were very complimentary as well. "Brilliant Pinner has Flying Start", was Brian Batty's headline in the *Daily Mail*. 'Pinner's darting runs and slick ball distribution left below-par Hull KR in a daze and he set the seal on a dazzling game with an inch-perfect pass to send Andy Platt strolling in for a fine try," wrote David Hodgkinson. So I must have been doing something right. Neil Barker in the *St Helens Star* thought that if my good form was to continue, I would actually be captain of the squad Down Under. Yet there were some critics who suggested that I was too small to be a successful loose-forward, so I was determined to prove them wrong and get on that plane.

We continued our good start with a win at Rochdale in the first round of the Lancashire Cup. In the second round at Knowsley Road, it was like open warfare when we met Warrington. Stan Wall was the referee and sent off five players – Roy Haggerty and Steve Peters from Saints and Phil Ford, Mal Yates and Mark Forster from the Wire. Stan also sent Mike Gregory and Bob Eccles to the sin bin, so how did we lose 30–26? Both teams were given suspended fines as a result of the brawling that took place. Warrington had a £1,000 fine hanging over them and we were done for £500.

We hit top form at home game to Bradford Northern, on 23 October, and beat a powerful side with a really tight defence 29–14. I thought I had controlled the game well and remember the display of a young second-rower called Paul Round, who came in for Peter Gorley, who was injured. He was another youngster who was coming through the ranks, who would only make us into a stronger team.

We started our run in the John Player Special trophy against Kent Invicta in Maidstone, who had the likes of Mark Elia in their team. We beat them fairly comfortably. By this time the club had done a two-way swap with Leeds. Gary Moorby went back to Yorkshire and we signed their front-rower Tony Burke in exchange. It was good business as far as I could see. Gary wanted to move back to Yorkshire and we got a real workhorse in exchange. He was such a durable player, who rarely got injured. He would always take the first ball up in a set, like Mel James, and he could run for a big lad – the sort of player we definitely wanted on our side.

After beating Warrington at Wilderspool 18–10 in round two, a much quieter affair than our first match, we won 16–12 against Featherstone Rovers to set up a semi-final tie with Widnes at Warrington 17 December. We had started to wear a different jersey design, with a much thicker red vee extending along the arms and this was the first match the shirts were sponsored, by St Helens Glass.

We had a disappointing Christmas and New Year, losing four on the bounce after the semi-final: Wigan on Boxing Day; Widnes at home on New Year's Day; Wakefield Trinity at Belle Vue and Hull at The Boulevard on 11 January. The defeat at Wakefield was particularly disappointing, because their new three-month signing from Australia, Wally Lewis seemed to beat us on one leg and scored a hat-trick of tries as well. I also remember we had a French referee for that game and he absolutely caned us in the penalty count. We did manage to perk up by hammering Whitehaven at Knowsley Road 40–10 and progressed into the second round of the Challenge Cup by beating Leigh, once again at home, to bring us up against a strong Hull side at home.

For me it was really important to do well because of tour selection and this was the platform to do it, with the BBC cameras there. Perhaps it was the time when our 'new' team would really start to show its worth and we could make a real bid for a place in the Challenge Cup final.

Watching the video of the game after so long made me realise what a good side we had developed into in many ways. Hull were a top team and it was never going to be easy. A young threequarter called Garry Schofield gave Hull the lead early on and could have scored a few more but for our cover-tackling. It was Steve Peters who turned provider for me to score just by the posts. I didn't think I had got there, originally, but watching it again there was no doubt about the try being given. Clive Griffiths converted and we were 6–4 up. Neil Holding was always a threat with his scurrying runs and gave a notable performance. He also could create and put Roy Haggerty in for our second converted try. I then just saw the opportunity to keep the scoreboard ticking over by putting over a couple of drop-goals, but Dannatt scored for Hull and our lead was down to four at half-time.

We managed to keep our lead; I put over another two 'drops' and we sealed the game with Neil Holding's second try, which Clive Griffiths converted. The final score was 24–14. It was a game I always felt we could dominate, especially with Neil's pace and Graham Liptrot's scrum domination and the way in which he bossed the area around the play-the-balls. We had willing workers in the forwards, with Tony Burke and Peter Gorley who were very difficult to pull down. There was also the pace of two of the younger lads in the back row, Andy Platt and Paul Round, who were always willing runners. Roundy, in particular, had a fine all-round game. Hull therefore missed out on a third successive Wembley appearance, although I felt sorry for their stand-off, Dave Topliss, who was a real class act.

I certainly had not done my own selection chances any harm. Arthur Brooks in the *Sunday Mirror* did quote me after the match and my frustrations at non-selection for Great Britain obviously came through: "I'm bitterly disappointed that I'm not in our British tour squad. It's not that I've played well today. I've been doing that for weeks. And I'm surprised that our international scrum-half Neil Holding isn't in it as well. He has been going great guns."

St Helens 18 Hull FC 8 (Challenge Cup), 25 February 1984.
Harry scored the vital try in this televised tie, despite some desperate Hull defence. He also kept the scoreboard ticking over with four drop-goals, to give Saints a home tie with Wigan in the next round. (Photo: Brian Peers)

St Helens 7 Wigan 16 (Challenge Cup), 11 March 1984
Day of destiny. Saints line up in pouring rain in front of over 20,000 fans. The subs were Johnny Smith and Shaun Allen. Back: Clive Griffiths, Tony Burke, Andy Platt, Paul Round, Peter Gorley, Chris Arkwright, Roy Haggerty; front: Steve Rule, Steve Peters, Harry Pinner (Capt) Graham Liptrot, Barry Ledger, Neil Holding. (Courtesy Alex Service)

Alan Thomas said I was "in complete control and a top class tactician ... the Saints' captain had led his team with authority and panache plus a massive personal contribution of four dropped goals, a try and a stream of precision passes." My four goals equalled the Challenge Cup record set by Johnny Blair of Halifax against Wakefield in 1980.

In the league, we had no realistic chance of the championship and so Wembley was our most important path for honours. The draw paired us with Wigan, who were gradually being rebuilt under coach Alex Murphy. Any Saints versus Wigan game generates interest among the supporters and this was no exception. The crowd at Knowsley Road was over 20,000, despite pouring rain. We were reasonably confident that we could beat them, but the pitch was obviously going to cut up later on.

On what was becoming a real mud heap we looked to have got the better of them and with 10 minutes to go, we were 7–4 up thanks to a brilliant Barry Ledger try on the Main Stand side. We had been 4–1 down at half-time. Unbelievably, the Wigan bench had been trying to get John Pendlebury substituted for several minutes when he popped up to score what proved to be the crucial try after a four-man move. Another try from their Australian stand-off Mark Cannon and two goals from Colin Whitfield meant that they went on to the semi-finals 16–7, where they played York, who had beaten Castleford. I was absolutely devastated at our second successive defeat in the quarter-finals at home, when the prospect of Wembley was not out of the question. As captain, I was upset with the way in which we had given up the advantage, but Wigan had their luck on the day, just when they needed it and for us, it was just another part of our learning curve as a team. Interviewed afterwards, Alex Murphy claimed that he had been very worried all week (nightmares in fact!) about my possible influence on the game, which was a back-handed compliment, but no consolation whatsoever.

The crowd of over 20,000 was the first at Knowsley Road since Murphy himself returned to Knowsley Road as a player with Leigh in the late 1960s. It was a great thrill to play in a typical derby atmosphere. We did improve our league form after the cup exit, with seven wins and a draw out of nine through to the end of the season, including a 20–13 victory over Wigan in the league at home on Good Friday, although the crowd was only 12,000 this time. I chipped through from about five yards and beating about four Wiganers to touch down – a brilliant moment. Another good win was against Oldham at Knowsley Road, when we won 31–20 after losing to them 32–6 at Watersheddings in early October, when their crowd gave us quite a bit of stick, with their 'easy, easy' chants. For Neil Holding and me it was a special game in that we celebrated our selection for the Australian tour, which I thought was never going to happen – certainly not for me. It was a lifetime's ambition to go on tour and I was determined to secure a test place. I was not going there for a holiday.

Back to club rugby, one of our most memorable victories was in the Premiership first round at Warrington, when we won 19–13. I seem to remember that we were down 3–2 at half-time before we got going and I dropped three goals to help us on our way. We finished in sixth place in the league and to beat the team in third place was a real achievement.

Paul Wilson's report gave me much credit, but his last line, when he talks about summer rugby league, is interesting:

Superb Pinner leaves sad Wires all cut up
Warrington 13 St Helens 19
By Paul Wilson

"'HP' said the announcer on the Wilderspool tannoy. He was not referring to hire purchase or the Houses of Parliament, though he could have added 'sauce'. Harry Pinner had just dropped his third goal in the space of about five minutes. Single-handedly, the St Helens skipper had taken the score on from 16–9 to 19–9 in Saints' favour, less than 10 minutes remained to play, and Warrington knew their chance had gone. What HP will achieve in Australia remains to be seen, but there's little doubt that he's currently the best number 13 operating on these shores.

Pinner left the field to an enormous cheer four minutes from time, even though he hadn't been directly involved in either of Saints' two decisive tries. He had been involved in just about everything else, of course, but what sticks in the mind is the nonchalant audacity of his three goals. The first was the best of the lot, a towering drive from fully 45 yards. Two more in as many minutes followed, from a little closer in, and Pinner finished his virtuoso show with an exemplary touch finder from the middle of the park. Goodness knows what [rugby union commentator] Bill McClaren and young Nigel [Starmer-Smith] would have made of it all. Pinner's heroics apart, this match was what most Premiership preliminaries are – a fairly unconvincing argument for summer rugby. (*Post and Chronicle* Monday, 30 April 1984)

We met our match in the semi-final against Hull KR at Craven Park, although I missed the game through injury. The lads held them early on, it was 9–6 at half-time, but then Rovers scored the crucial try. So a season of what might have been. I played 34 matches, scored four tries and kicked 14 drop-goals. Other lads who played over 30 matches included: Peter Gorley, Barry Ledger, Steve Rule, Graham Liptrot, Neil Holding, Roy Haggerty, Tony Burke and Andy Platt, who established himself in the side. The 'Sleeping Giant' – St Helens RFC – was coming back to life. We needed a marquee player to put us into contention. He was a real problem for the Lions in Australia – Mal Meninga.

6. Behind the bar

"Rugby league is quite simply a way of life to Harry Pinner. He's landlord of the Victoria Hotel, Newton-le-Willows and the home of a sporting winner hits you immediately."
Neil Barker

A drink with the Lions

I have in my possession a menu for the Annual British Lions Association reunion luncheon for 1988 and it included a list of famous playing members of the Association, who had taken out an advert for their own public houses:
Ram's Head, Haydock (Willie Aspinall); Griffin Hotel, Wigan (Billy Boston); Rosebud Inn (Keith Bridges); Mexborough Arms, Castleford (Bill Bryant); Half Moon Hotel, Hull (Len Casey); King William Hotel, Hull (Peter Flanagan); Derby Arms, Rainford (Kenny Gill); Woodman Inn, York (Dennis Goodwin); Dick Turpin Hotel, York (Tommy Harris); Zetland Arms, Hull (Colin Hutton); Navigation Inn, Wakefield (Brian Lockwood); Bridge Hotel, Burtonwood (Roy Mathias); Grayrigge Hotel, Grange-Over Sands (Reg Parker); Royal Oak Hotel, Hull (Paul Rose); Goodman Hotel, Hunslet (Paul Rose); Brook House inn, Wigan (John Stopford); Prospect Inn (Ken Traill); Piece Hall Hotel, Halifax (Jack Wilkinson); Golden Lion, Ferrybridge (John Ward); Eureka Club, Hull (Johnny Whiteley); Black Bull Hotel, Mawdesley (Dave Willicombe) Big Jim's Night Club, Widnes (Jim Mills).

In the old days it was a recognised fact that many rugby league and football players capitalised on their popularity by keeping pubs. I can remember my dad talking about Saints' centre Duggie Greenall (Engine Inn, Parr and Talbot Hotel) and Ken Large (Victoria Hotel, Rainhill). One of the most successful licensees was the great Alf Ellaby, another member of the Lions' Association, who kept the Veevers Arms and later the Ardwick Hotel in Blackpool. Needless to say, they were popular places to visit for Saints fans in particular and extremely busy with the holiday trade right up to the end of the illuminations.

I had always wanted to become a licensee and trained to be a publican at the Black Horse, in Moss Bank for a spell, just to learn the ropes. It was obviously more appealing than pipe-laying for the council, but I was under no illusions that it would be hard work and my life would not be my own with the long hours involved. Lawrie Prescott, a Saints director – and later chairman – worked for Greenall Whitley and said he would help us to fulfil what was a real ambition.

On the lawn at the back of the Victoria Hotel, with the locals and my mum and dad. This photo was also in Harry's Testimonial brochure in 1985.
(Courtesy Harry Pinner)

We waited for a few months and the brewery offered us a few pubs, but then a vacancy arose, at the Victoria Pub in Wargrave Road, Newton-le-Willows and we took over the lease. We must have liked a challenge.

The Victoria was somewhat run down and had an old bowling green. We cut the green and made it into a play area for kids. Eventually we were able to have barbeques for up to 150 people.

Wendy and I were living in Paisley Avenue, Blackbrook, in a bungalow. Needless to say we were delighted to take over the tenancy, but it was a little strange at first, moving outside St Helens. We soon found our feet there, as it happened and it became a place where rugby league was always the topic of discussion over a drink, or two. We lived in the pub and made a real success of it. We had a really good mix of supporters. Don't forget from where we were in Newton, St Helens, Warrington and Wigan were each about five miles away. The pub did well before and after matches with rugby league fans. When we first went in, we were lucky to be doing five kegs. By the time we left, we would be doing 30 kegs.

Christmas and New Year were the busiest times for us and for me in particular. I would be closing late on Christmas night with the Boxing Day derby against Wigan the following day. Perhaps not the best preparation. Then, of course, it was New Year's Eve – a really late finish and a game against Widnes the following afternoon. We had to be wary of any possible trouble brewing late on during the evening, especially on public holiday nights, although I felt that I could handle any of that stuff. It was part and parcel of being a licensee as far as I understood it. After

64

test match rugby league against the likes of Kurt Sorenson and Mark Graham it was not too difficult to deal with an awkward customer.

A rocky road ahead

Life in a public house can provide some freedom and flexibility if there are reliable staff to cover and it was a good thing for me, as a rugby league player, both in terms of being able to go to training and matches and also the fact that the pub, as I said, became a bit of a magnet for rugby league people. Unfortunately, there are some inevitable stresses and strains and by the mid-1980s, my marriage to Wendy was at an end. It was a painful time for both of us and, for me, it coincided with the Saints actually beginning to fulfil their potential as a team now capable of challenging for major honours, so a bitter-sweet feeling in many ways.

We did not have any children and I kept the tenancy of the Victoria on, with lots of help from friends and family, although I was starting again from scratch and there was lots of hard work still to be put in.

We had a big celebration at the Victoria the day after we had won the Lancashire Cup in 1984, when all the team came over. It was at that memorable event that I first bumped into Anne Creighton. She was the sister of Geoff Cropper's wife Lillian. Geoff, a prominent cricketer, had become a valued friend, who helped me as secretary of my Testimonial Committee. Anne lived in Eliza Street, in Sutton and, like me, was coming out of a previous relationship. But first things first. I needed help behind the bar and had advertised for barmaids without success. Anne said she could do it on a regular basis, which was ideal for me and I took her on.

She was a really good help for the pub and, to cut a long story short, romance blossomed and we were married at St Helens Registry Office in February 1989. It was through links with the licensing trade that we bought our thatched cottage, at Appleton Thorn just outside Warrington, where we lived for 30 years. The opportunity arose when Frank Karalius, Vinty's brother, who was at the Railway Hotel in Garswood, gave us a call one Christmas Day saying he had run out of beer. We sorted him out and he said later that there would be an opportunity to buy this cottage – and we took it. It was a perfect place for us and over the years we developed it as the perfect place for our bulldogs in particular.

We also bought the lease to another Greenall Whitley pub, the Parr Arms in Church Lane in Grappenhall in the early 1990s. It was obviously quite sad to leave the Victoria behind, but this was a new challenge for us, in a totally different area. The main difference was that we would do more on the catering side and provide pub meals. The Victoria was a traditional ale pub in the best sense, so this was a real change for us, but I'd like to think we succeeded. It was really busy, especially at holiday times and weekends, and things could be quite stressful at times.

Obviously it wasn't in a traditional rugby league area, although there were lots of Warrington fans in the Grappenhall area.

In the end we enjoyed 14 years at the Parr Arms, before retiring in 2007. It was very hard work, but a great experience. We won a couple of awards at the Parr Arms for our food, so maybe that was a measure of what we put into the business. We both enjoyed ourselves and made a number of friends and acquaintances, but it was the right time to go in the end. When we finished I gave my rugby memorabilia away to our customers and, maybe I regret not keeping a few mementoes.

One thing about a pub is that the landlord is only as good as their staff and we were very lucky in that respect. I would also like to add that I will be forever grateful to my mum and dad for the help they gave in running the Victoria, in particular, when I was on tour or during the general routine of training and matches.

In the meanwhile, our daughter Joanne was born in October 1989, while we were still in the Vic. She has been the apple of our eyes ever since and, with children of her own now, she gave us another source of happiness as grandparents. Who would have thought it? Pub life seems a long way away these days.

7. Disaster Down Under

"Pinner must have returned from the tour disillusioned and confused, but his response to adversity said much about his character and attitude: 'I'm not the sort of person to say I'm taking my ball home.'"
Paul Fitzpatrick

To be selected for a Lions tour of Australia and New Zealand was the ultimate ambition for any British rugby league player in the 1980s, just as it had always been since the first-ever tour Down Under in 1910. I was brought up on tales of some of the great Saints players who went on tour, such as Alf Ellaby before the war; Alan Prescott, Alex Murphy, Cliff Watson, John Mantle and, of course, my first rugby league idol, Duggie Laughton, although when he went on tour, in 1970, he was a Wigan player.

But Duggie was part of something very special that year: Great Britain had won the Ashes on Australian soil. Now that was the ultimate achievement in my book. The captain of the 1970 Lions was Frank Myler, who was also a St Helens player and, 14 years later, he was appointed coach of the Great Britain squad that would, once again, play three test matches each in both Australia and New Zealand. I was absolutely made up to be on that plane.

It had been a shock for all of us when the 1982 Kangaroos went through unbeaten on their own tour of Britain and France. Things had to change in a lot of ways if we were ever to regain the Ashes after that. The game needed to become more professional in its outlook all round. There was one thing that was in our favour. The Brits were always renowned for their ball-playing ability at the expense, maybe, of power and strength. Perhaps these last two aspects in particular were the key to success at international level.

Being in the Great Britain squad, it was a tremendous step-up in intensity and competition for places was fierce. I always had confidence in my ability as a ball-player and, eventually, as a leader at international level, but here I was selected for the tour which was going to be a whole new experience.

As I said earlier, I was a rather late inclusion in the 1984 squad and had not been a part of the get-togethers and training camps that the other lads had attended. Chris Arkwright was selected and then dramatically withdrawn just days later and everyone at Saints really felt for him. He was a rising star and certainly not out of place at test match level. He was brought in as one of the original replacements for players who were injured or suspended, with Hull's Wayne Proctor. Chris failed a late fitness test and was replaced by Oldham's Terry Flanagan.

Great Britain photo call: Part of the line-up of the squad at the Sydney Cricket Ground. Left to right: Terry Flanagan, Steve Donlan, Harry Pinner, Keith Mumby, Neil Holding and Andy Gregory. Harry doesn't look too happy; perhaps he had a premonition of disappointing times ahead. (Courtesy Alex Service)

The tour squad was as follows:
Brian Noble (captain, Bradford Northern)
Backs: Ray Ashton (Oldham), Mick Burke (Widnes), Garry Clark (Hull KR), Steve Donlan (Leigh), Des Drummond (Leigh), Ronnie Duane (Warrington), Des Foy (Oldham), Andy Gregory (Widnes), Ellery Hanley (Bradford Northern), Neil Holding (St Helens), John Joyner (Castleford), Joe Lydon (Widnes), Keith Mumby (Bradford Northern), Tony Myler (Widnes), Garry Schofield (Hull), Mike Smith (Hull KR)
Forwards: Mick Adams (Widnes), Kevin Beardmore (Castleford), Chris Burton (Hull KR), Brian Case (Wigan), Lee Crooks (Hull), Terry Flanagan (Oldham), Andy Goodway (Oldham), David Hobbs (Featherstone Rovers), Mike O'Neill (Widnes), Harry Pinner (St Helens), Wayne Proctor (Hull), Keith Rayne (Leeds), Mick Worrall (Oldham).

1984 Australian tour matches

Northern Territory 13 Great Britain 40
18 May 1984, Richardson Park, Darwin
I played in the first game of the tour and thought I did well. I think the majority of us were still recovering from jet lag. The temperature was in the 80s, which didn't help either. I can remember that Neil Holding came on for Ray Ashton after 54 minutes and our back three was: Worrall, Hobbs and Pinner. I really did think that I could have 'kicked on' from

there, but my biggest rival for a test place was Mick Adams from Widnes, who, of course, was a really great player. In fact, he was my room-mate during the tour itself and there was never a feeling of animosity between us. We always seemed to get on really well.

Great Britain scorers:

Tries: Noble (2), Goodway (2), Donlan, Drummond, Hanley, Foy.

Goals: Crooks (3), Hobbs

Western Division 30 Great Britain 36

27 May 1984, Victoria Park, Dubbo

I was replaced by David Hobbs after 57 minutes. Our back three was: Burton, Hobbs and Pinner. Great Britain were 30–26 down with 11 minutes left, having led 18–2 early in the first half. The heat and a series of penalties went against the tourists, who were 22–14 up at half-time.

Great Britain scorers:

Tries: Foy (3), Crooks, Ashton, Noble, Mumby.

Goals: Burke (4).

Newcastle 18 Great Britain 28

2 June 1984, International Sports Centre

I came off the bench for Lee Crooks after half-time. Our back three was: Hobbs, Worrall and Flanagan. An 11,000 crowd saw the tourists again hammered in the penalty count, with the referee criticised by the Australians for his handling of the match.

By this stage we also had a growing injury list. However, this win meant we were unbeaten before the first test.

Great Britain scorers:

Tries: Schofield, Flanagan, Hanley, Holding, Clark.

Goals: Burke (4)

Wide Bay 18 Great Britain 28

11 June 1984, Salter Oval, Bundaberg

The referee started the match in a red shirt, the same as the home team. He changed it for a blue one after 14 minutes. I was replaced by Mick Worrall after 65 minutes. Our back three was: Proctor, Flanagan and Pinner. The penalties went 21–7 against the tourists, which prevented us building any rhythm. Kevin Beardmore was sin-binned for failing to get onside.

This was our first match after the first test at the Sydney Cricket Ground, which we lost 25–8.

Great Britain scorers:

Tries: Hanley, Proctor, Beardmore, Basnett, Worrall.

Goals: Lydon (4).

North Queensland 20 Great Britain 38

17 June 1984; Townsville

The match was refereed by Barry Gomersall, and played in humid heat. Our back three was: O'Neill, Proctor and Pinner. We were 24–6 up at half-time.

Great Britain scorers:

Tries: Hanley (2), Drummond (2), Beardmore, Smith, Basnett.

Goals: Lydon (5)

Toowoomba 18 Great Britain 16

20 June 1984; Athletic Oval

Our back three was: Proctor, Hobbs and Pinner. We were 12–4 down at half-time, got back to 12–10 before they scored to go 18–10 ahead. We pulled back their lead with a converted try near the end. Most of the side had played three days before.

Great Britain scorers:

Tries: Basnett, Clark, Smith.

Goals: Hobbs (2)

Northern Rivers 12 Great Britain 24

28 June 1984; Tweed Heads

Our back three was: Proctor, Hobbs and Pinner. This match was two days after our 18–6 defeat in Brisbane in the second test. We were 16–2 ahead when Joe Lydon was sent off in the 44th minute. The home team abused the substitute rules, making 10 changes.

Great Britain scorers:

Tries: Clark, Drummond, Hobbs, Smith.

Goals: Lydon (2), Hobbs (2).

Before the second test I also caught flu. Chris Burton was the same and we were in the same room with an 'unclean' sign on the door. Obviously, there were some moments that were very funny when there are such a number of lads staying together away from home for so long. Some stories are downright unprintable, as 'what happens on tour stays on tour' but perhaps one surprising thing is that I ended up sleeping with Andy Gregory. Please let me explain.

Greg was having a hard time getting to sleep because of his team-mate Lee Crooks's extra loud snoring and he came to our room and asked if he could stay. Basically, he slept with his face plastered against the side wall, although it did seem to do the trick and he got a better night's sleep.

We stayed for a spell at the Sheraton in Sydney and one thing I remember is that there was an old couple who had fallen asleep on a settee in the foyer. Needless to say they were lifted up – settee and all

– by several Great Britain tourists and put in the nearest lift. God knows what happened to them after that. The ice dancers Torville and Dean were in the same hotel, but we didn't see much of them. Perhaps they were wise enough to avoid us.

Looking back, I suppose that Frank Myler wanted me to be more physical as a player. Although I would never shirk any of the physical stuff, it was not easy, as I wasn't the biggest loose forward in the international game. My biggest strength has always been with ball in hand and laying off passes for others. On the tour one thing I thought was strange was that many players were playing out of position throughout the team, which didn't really do us much good in the long term. There was some criticism about my tackling, but there was no use in making 40 tackles in a game without doing anything with the ball.

I did think that I had improved my tackling technique overall during my career and have never let anyone down in terms of effort, but my biggest asset is as a ball-player.

It was bad enough being what they call a Ham and Egger for quite a number of the games that I was forced to miss through injury – especially the tests. In the end Mick Adams was the first-choice loose-forward. As for Neil Holding, at least he did manage to play in the tests at some stage, although he too had injury problems. It was so disappointing, gut-wrenching in fact, to have to be told that you would be on the plane home on 27 July, with 11 matches still to go, including the New Zealand leg of the tour and no test match appearances. I was joined on the plane by Ray Ashton and Garry Schofield.

The actual injury was around the hamstring area and let's just say it didn't quite respond to treatment. Even today I can feel an almond-shaped knot where the original injury was. In the end, I had to see a specialist in Manchester called Fred Griffiths. He had been Manchester City's physio and now had a private practice in St. John Street. He eventually treated the injury successfully, but it was about 13 weeks before I felt anything like my normal self. Interestingly, one of his patients at the time was the Manchester United centre-half Gordon McQueen, who, I believe, had a similar long-standing injury.

I remember telling an Australian journalist that I was bitterly disappointed with the way things had gone. I genuinely thought I could get into the test side, but as it turned out, I was injured for four of the eight weeks I was there and some of the injuries and illness coincided with the test matches. Despite the disappointment, it was a fantastic experience to play rugby in places I had only read about in travel brochures or geography books. Two places I played at are now the home of NRL clubs: Newcastle (Knights) and Townsville (North Queensland Cowboys) and Bundaberg is the birthplace of Mal Meninga.

71

An article by Paul Fitzpatrick, of *The Guardian* summed up my tour and frustrations to a tee: "One always felt that that Frank Myler the coach and Dick Gemmell the manager included him in their squad in response to a strong press lobby rather than out of a conviction of his talents. That feeling strengthened on a tour which was to prove a big disappointment for Pinner. He was not chosen for any of the Tests in Australia and NZ and eventually he was forced to return home early because of injury. In the minor games which he did play he was frequently asked to fill roles alien to his style and there were even instances when he was clinging hold of the ball and driving into the tackle as first man. Pinner must have returned from the tour disillusioned and confused, but his response to adversity said much about his character and attitude: 'I'm not the sort of person to say I'm taking my ball home.'"

I still had faith in my own ability and when I returned home I was more determined than ever to continue to play well at club level for Saints. Maybe I would return to test rugby in the future, with the Kiwis coming over in 1985–86, but nothing in sport is certain.

8. The Crowning Glory

"No-one argues with Harry when he bears his gums and points an accusing finger Tommy Smith-style. My abiding memory of the Lancashire Cup final was such a scene as the team left the dressing room before that historic match with Wigan. Without the four-letter words it wasn't a very long speech, but roughly translated Harry made it clear that he wouldn't tolerate anything less than total commitment. He wanted that cup so badly it hurt."
Elton Welsby

When it was first known that Saints were chasing a top Australian player and that he would obviously be on much more money than any of the lads – skipper included – it did cause some initial ructions and rumblings, especially from the local players. I remember saying to them that it will certainly increase our chances of winning trophies and there would be more winning money for all of us as a result.

It was like what has been proposed in the current Super League competition, where each club can have a 'marquee player'. In the end, they were all right about it and having the players like Mal Meninga and some of the other Australian imports, although they were short-term, certainly had a positive effect on our players in terms of their sheer professionalism and the way they trained and approached games, not just at Saints, but throughout the league as a whole.

It was also another attraction for the supporters, to see great players like Meninga, Sterling, Kenny, Grothe and so on, still at their peak. Not as it can be today when Australian stars look towards coming to England to enhance their pension pots. It doesn't mean that they are not committed, but that we are not seeing them at their best.

I genuinely felt that in 1984–85 we were strong contenders for honours. The Meninga signing did create tremendous interest in the town and there was a real buzz around Knowsley Road. As captain I was really looking forward to the new campaign, although there would be one or two hiccups along the way. It wouldn't be Saints without any, would it?

Training was basically at the ground on Tuesday nights. This was quite an important part of our preparation and we had a time when we went to the Astroturf pitch at Boundary Road on Thursdays, which was quite hard on my legs. At one stage, a sprint coach, Brian Green, was brought in. Pace was very important, of course and I could see why. Our coach, Billy Benyon, was a real fitness fanatic and expected everyone else to be as committed as he was and trained with us.

Tuesday was when we did weights at the back of the stand and reviewed the previous week's match. Saturday morning was when we put all our tactical moves together for the following day's match, pretty much the same as the captain's run that the current team do. Training was in full view of the spekkies at Knowsley Road and there was a fair crowd of regulars turning up to watch us on the training pitch. One guy, John Morgan, who was getting on a bit, always seemed to be there. The Supporters Club used to sell drinks on the colder evenings.

We began the season without Mal with three straight wins, at home to Featherstone, away to Leeds and beat Runcorn in the first round of the Lancashire Cup. A new player made his debut at Leeds and seemed to be confident as a goalkicker. His name was Sean Day and he ended the season top of the charts. He was a brilliant kicker and definitely one reason why we could now compete for major honours. We made further progress against Barrow in the Lancashire Cup, but had a reality check with two defeats at Hull KR and Bradford, conceding over 60 points in the two matches.

The stage was set for the debut of Mal Meninga, with the visit of Castleford at Knowsley Road. There were over 8,000 fans there, which was a big improvement on what we had been getting over the past few seasons. We didn't have much time to familiarise ourselves with him in training, but it was obvious. If he got the ball in anything like space out wide, he would be really very difficult to stop in full flight. As it happened, Mal did just that and scored twice. There was a lot of interest in the game with his debut and we also had Phil Veivers at full-back for the first time, the so-called 'makeweight' in the Meninga deal. Talking of weight, some people thought that Mal was overweight and out of condition. He was to prove the critics wrong by a mile.

Although Phil didn't quite set the world on fire in his first match, Billy Benyon kept him in for the next game against Leigh in the Lancashire Cup semi-final – we won 31–10 – and he had a blinder. One of his main strengths was to defuse high kicks. These 'bombs' were now becoming an even more important part of the game and I had been putting the ball up myself on the last tackle for many years, leading to Graham Liptrot's try at Wembley in 1978.

Cup Kings of Lancashire

It certainly seemed as though Mal had increased the confidence of the team overall and we then went on a 13-game unbeaten run. On 28 October we had our first major test as a team when we played Wigan in the Lancashire Cup Final. There was terrific interest in the game. Wigan were on a bit of a roll like us, but what made it more difficult was that we lost the toss for home advantage. So in the wind and pouring rain we walked out at Central Park in front of 26,074 fans – a huge crowd. This was our big stage and we desperately wanted to win for those Saints fans who had been starved of success since the late 1970s.

Considering the conditions, we played some brilliant rugby in the first half. We managed to keep the line moving and got Wigan on the back foot for most of the time. Needless to say we wanted to concentrate our attack on the left hand side with Meninga the key to our attacking plans. After about six minutes, we got a tap penalty just outside the Wigan '25' line. Tony Burke did his usual 'first man in' plunge. Neil Holding gave it to Lippy and then shot away left, with the ball going to the blind side, where we got Meninga away. Wigan winger John Ferguson took Mal's dummy and Mal powered his way over.

It was obvious then that if we kept doing this, they would find it difficult to cope. We continued to put the ball through the hands and our two second-rowers, Andy Platt and Paul Round were putting the Wiganers under pressure with their pace out wide. I dropped a difficult pass – I think I over-ran it – that would have given us a big overlap, but we still continued to attack them with everything we had.

Andy Platt got the ball out wide and put it inside for Round, who was tackled short of the line. Mal came in at acting half and gave it to Roy Haggerty, who had come on as a sub for Phil Veivers, and scored a brilliant try on the burst.

The conversion gave us a 12–2 lead – something that I really didn't think we would have at this stage of the match. And it became more. When Wigan lost the ball, five minutes later, we scored again. The ball went down the line to Mal once again and he put Sean Day in for another one in the corner. Sean kicked the goal as well and we were really buzzing now, at 18–2.

We continued to dominate territory and possession and I made sure we moved the ball out wide as often as possible. I tried to break through down the middle and the ball was moved wide by Holding and round to Big Mal, who ran at the young full-back, Shaun Edwards, who had no chance of stopping him. Sean Day kicked another touchline conversion and there we were, after our third try in nine minutes, with a 24–2 lead. We jogged off at half-time very satisfied with our performance, but we knew that the second half would be more difficult, especially if Wigan got more possession, with the crowd behind them.

Sure enough, we found ourselves under pressure after half-time and it literally became a game of two halves. They managed to score three tries. Henderson Gill got the first, from a kick from one of their Australians, Mark Cannon and then Graeme West got through three tacklers. I won't tell you what I said after that one, but the air was blue. Cannon kicked again and Nicky Kiss scored after another scramble, but we managed to keep our eight-point advantage thanks to a Sean Day penalty – our only points of the half.

St Helens 30 Castleford 16, 7 October 1984. Getting the team moving against Castleford, when Mal Meninga made his debut for Saints. The crowd was double its normal size – 7,366. (Courtesy Alex Service)

St Helens 26 Wigan 18, 1984 Lancashire Cup Final at Central Park, Harry lifts his first trophy as Saints' captain. Barry Ledger on the right, gives him a hand. Eric Ashton is above Barry, in the white mac. (Photo: Brian Peers)

It was a brilliant feeling when the final hooter went and Mal Meninga got a well-deserved Man-of-the-Match award. In the first half we had played brilliantly and certainly deserved to win overall, given the fact that we were the away team on the day. The champagne and beer flowed in the dressing room afterwards and we all felt pretty pleased with our achievements.

Billy Benyon was delighted and wanted it to be just the start of what could be further success with our team that was the perfect blend of youth and experience. We were playing attractive rugby and on the day, we thought we could beat anyone. It was Saints' first major honour since 1977 and we were all very proud to have been a part of it.

Both county cup finals took place on the same day in front of huge crowds. Over in Yorkshire it was the Humberside derby, with Hull hammering Hull KR 29–12 at Hull City's ground in front of 25,237 fans. Apart from Wigan, the biggest threat would come from Humberside, especially from Rovers, although Leeds and Oldham were strong contenders as well.

Lancashire Cup final
St Helens (24) 26 Wigan (2) 18
28 October 1984
Central Park, Wigan
St Helens: Veivers; Ledger, Allen, Meninga (2T), Day (1T 5G); Arkwright, Holding; Burke, Liptrot, Gorley, Platt, Round, Pinner (Capt). Subs: Smith, Haggerty (1T)
Wigan: Edwards; Ferguson, Stephenson, Whitfield (3G), Gill (1T); Cannon, Fairhurst; Courtney, Kiss (1T), Case, West (Capt 1T), Wane, Potter. Subs: Pendlebury, Scott
Man of the Match: Mal Meninga (St Helens)
Referee: Ron Campbell (Widnes)
Attendance: 26,074

We won our next match, against Warrington in the league and at the end of November we faced Bradford Northern at Odsal in the John Player Trophy. We had already played them at home in the league the week before and won, but this was going to be more difficult. They had a new star in Ellery Hanley, who was really making a name for himself. It was always awkward to play there because of the curled up corners of the pitch as a result of the speedway track. It was a really hard game and two tries – one from Hanley, the other from Barry Ledger – were down to the curled up corners. Unfortunately, we had to do without Roy Haggerty just before half-time when he 'coat-hangered' Bradford's Alan Rathbone. It was 12–12 and they were creeping towards our line for a drop-goal when the hooter went.

Saints with the Lancashire Cup before the John Player Trophy match against Keighley at Knowsley Road. Back: Phil Veivers, Paul Round, Peter Gorley, Mal Meninga, Roy Haggerty, Andy Platt; middle: Eric Leach (kit man), Graham Liptrot, Harry Pinner (Capt), Tony Burke, Steve Peters, Shaun Allen; front: Denis Litherland, Sean Day, Neil Holding, Barry Ledger. (Photo: Brian Peers)

In the replay, three days later at Saints, Rathbone played and we had another man – Andy Platt – sent off, this time for alleged biting, once again just before the interval. We won 24–10; Neil Holding scored twice, but both games really took it out of us.

The following Sunday we hit Leeds with a 32-point blitz in the second half to win 48–16, which is one of the games many people remember from the 'Meninga Season'. Chris Arkwright was on fire that day and scored a hat-trick of tries.

The wheels sort of fell off after that match. We lost 14–8 in the next round of the John Player competition to Halifax at Knowsley Road and there were rumours going round that one or two of the team had been going out socially maybe a bit once too often. It certainly was a shock result and the board saw fit to impose a 'booze ban' on us. It is true that some of the lads liked a night out and were quite regular night-clubbers, but it was the start of a bad spell for us. From going 13 games unbeaten when Mal first arrived, we lost six out of 10 from Boxing Day to early March. Our opening match in the Challenge Cup was with Hull KR and the fixture was called off a few times because of the snowy conditions and eventually played on 21 February. They battered Meninga every time he got the ball and we lost 8–3.

It was a disappointing time, because we had all wanted a good cup run to get to Wembley, but it wasn't to be. What's more, we lost Lippy again with his fourth broken jaw, after a difficult game at Featherstone. The ground had seen better days and that part of Yorkshire was in turmoil as a result of the miners strike and was not the best place to be. The club signed Leigh's Gary Ainsworth to fill the gap and although he wasn't as good at getting the ball from the scrums as Lippy, he was quite lively in the loose and did a really good job for us.

He made his debut in a 19–19 draw at Halifax, who had a load of Australians playing for them, including Chris Anderson and Martin Bella. Our losing streak ended after a defeat at Oldham on 8 March and we only lost one more game before the end-of-season Premiership. We did have a chance of winning the league at one stage, when we beat Wigan at Central Park 30–19 and Hull KR at Knowsley Road 30–14. However, in the end, Hull KR won two games more than we did and we lost the First Division title by three points.

The Premiership was our last chance for silverware, particularly for Big Mal who was due back home in May. The first round game against Widnes was televised at Knowsley Road and we won fairly easily, but Wigan were waiting for us in round two, after their Challenge Cup Final success against Hull. As it happened, it was one of those great nights at Knowsley Road. It was close until after half-time and we went on to beat them 37–14. We scored 20 points in the last 15 minutes as Wigan tired. I managed to score one of the tries and kick a drop-goal to help to clinch the victory. Our supporters went wild and the noise was unbelievable.

People said that Wigan's Brett Kenny wasn't too bothered about the game after the triumph at Wembley, but don't believe it. He wanted to win just like everyone else. In terms of league positions, first – Hull KR – and second – Saints – were in the final, which was held at Elland Road. Given that Hull KR had won the First Division title, we were the underdogs on the day. They had a big, strong pack and a good back line, but we were still confident that we could beat them and prevent them getting a second successive Championship and Premiership double. Although they had lost their key Australian signing loose forward Gavin Miller through injury, they were still a brilliant team.

We began in style, trying to play what we were good at – fast, open rugby. We scored some fantastic team tries in a really open game. There wasn't a bad player in a blue Saints jersey. Apart from Mal's two interceptions, Barry Ledger scored two cracking tries and I virtually walked one in when the whole Rovers defence took the dummy. The video shows what it meant to me. The trophy was ours.

St Helens 36 Hull KR 16, 1985 Premiership final at Elland Road
Feeling confident and running the show. (Courtesy Alex Service)

Left: The score says it all. Harry lifted on high at Elland Road by Barry Ledger and Tony Burke. (Photo: Brian Peers)

Celebrating with the Premiership trophy at Elland Road. Steve Peters and Neil Holding (front) seem to be really enjoying the moment. (Courtesy Alex Service)

I had won another trophy and the Harry Sunderland Trophy for Man-of-the-Match in my 300th game for the club. It didn't really come much better than that – certainly the highlight of my career at Saints.

Premiership final
St Helens (22) 36 Hull KR (14) 16
11 May 1985
Elland Road, Leeds
St Helens: Veivers (1T); Ledger (2T), Peters, Meninga (2T), Day (4G); Arkwright, Holding; Burke, Ainsworth (1T), Gorley, Platt, Haggerty, Pinner (Capt 1T). Subs: Forber, Allen
Hull KR: Fairbairn (1T 2G); Clark, Robinson (1T), Prohm, Laws (1T); Mike Smith, Gordon Smith; Broadhurst, Watkinson (Capt), Ema, Kelly, Hogan, Hall. Subs: Lydiat, Harkin.
Harry Sunderland Trophy: Harry Pinner (St Helens)
Referee: Stan Wall (Leigh)
Attendance: 15,518

It was a proud moment to receive the famous Harry Sunderland Trophy. Since it was first awarded in 1965, I was the fifth Saint to receive it. Albert Halsall was the first in 1966; Frank Myler won it in 1970 and two players who became my team-mates when I came into the First Team also received the award: George Nicholls in 1976 and Geoff Pimblett the following year. Definitely not bad company to be in. A few months later, Brian Batty wrote these words in an article in my Testimonial brochure: "No-one could under-estimate Mal Meninga's mighty contribution, but the man who bossed the show, master-minding Saints' attacking moves as they rained in the tries was ....Pinner."

It had certainly been an exhausting season at club level and was not over yet. I made 35 appearances during the season and others who managed to do over 30 were: Shaun Allen, Tony Burke (42!) Peter Gorley, Sean Day, Roy Haggerty, Neil Holding, Barry Ledger, Mal Meninga, and Andy Platt. Shaun Allen's best position at the time was in the centre and he was a really good club man. Tony Burke was our 'first man in' who would drive it in on the opening tackle of a set. He had really deceptive pace as well and would never let anybody down, a really solid footballer.

Sean Day, as I said before, excelled with his goalkicks and topped the goalkicking and points-scoring charts, the first player to do that since Geoff Pimblett and Kel Coslett. Peter Gorley was a typical raw-boned Cumbrian forward, all knees and elbows. Roy Haggerty played more in the second row, rather than as a centre and it was the making of him. He knew when I wanted him to run off me and he never, ever, bottled out. He had this amazing juddering run and side-step. A natural footballer? No ... but so effective in his own way. The spekkies loved him.

Neil Holding always seemed to play well in the televised games they had at the time, as part of Granada TVs *RL Action*. Elton Welsby was the host and he always watched the team whenever he could. Neil was, as I have said before, a great support player and my advice to any scrum-half today with pace – watch him on video, especially his 'chip and chase'.

Perhaps Barry Ledger was never the supreme athlete – he liked a drink and a smoke – but was a natural winger, with a fantastic swerve, as well as pace. He always looked elegant when running with the ball and scored a shedful of tries. Mal Meninga scored 28 tries himself and remains a truly world class player in my eyes. You name it, he could do it. He is the best centre I have played with or against, a consummate professional who the lads looked up to. As for Andy Platt, he was a fine wide-running second-rower who could really dump his opponent in the tackle. Andy was another who used to thrive off my passes. I always saw him as a back-rower and was surprised when he was moved to the front-row, but he did the business there as well.

These guys made over 30 appearances, but there were others who made some brilliant contributions, like Chris Arkwright, who played for Great Britain when I captained the side against the Kiwis in 1985–86, a real powerhouse and so effective wherever he played. Steve Peters was another great club man at centre. Not many got past him and he was a really solid player. Paul Round was Platt's partner in the second row and another fearless runner who I could try and put through the gap. He came on to the ball well and was quite fearless, playing above his size.

 Paul could be a bit headstrong and I had to keep him in his place at times, but that's what a captain's for, isn't it? Paul Forber was another former colt who had come into the first team and proved his worth. He was a real bustling forward, who showed no fear when taking the ball up and was a good team player.

I also need to mention, once again, our full-back, Phil Veivers, who trained well and dealt brilliantly with any high kicks. He knew when to join the line and ran the ball out well – a real asset to the team and remained so for many years! As for Billy Benyon, he initially rejected a one-year contract offer because he wanted a new three year contract. In the end, there was a compromise and the club gave him a two-year deal. Needless to say we were all pleased that Billy remained our coach.

We knew in April that our season would be extended by a four match tour of New Zealand. It was a terrific experience for us and great for team spirit. The club got special jerseys for us, sponsored by Pilkingtons, and club blazers, so we really felt it was a pleasure to represent our team and the town. Chairman John Clegg was in charge of the party, with Bill Lyon his assistant. We flew over a fortnight after the Premiership Final and played our first game against Canterbury on 26 May.

A photoshoot for the 1985 New Zealand tour with our specially-designed jerseys, sponsored by Pilkingtons. Unfortunately, Mal Meninga didn't join Saints in New Zealand. He would have been a big attraction for their fans.
(Photo: Brian Peers)

Our other games were against Waikato on 29 May, Manukau on 2 June and Northland on the following day. These were area representative teams, except for the Manukau Magpies. Apart from the Premiership-winning squad, we also brought along lads who had contributed well during the season, like scrum-half Johnny Smith, full-back Kevin Wellens and a young lad who was to become a Great Britain player in his own right – Paul Loughlin. Mal Meninga had returned to play for Canberra and he would have been a big drawing card for us on the tour.

Our first game against Canterbury was tough, just as we expected it and they had some familiar names in their team such as Brent Todd and Adrian Shelford. We lost 30–24 and also went down by the same score to Waikato at Huntly three days later. On 2 June we played the Lion Red Manukau Magpies, whose coach was Dean Bell's father, Cameron, with Kelly Shelford and Clayton Friend in the halves. They were the top team in the First Division and the league's leading try-scorer was Mark Elia, of Te Atatu, who joined Saints before the 1985–86 season was over. Manukau Magpies turned us over 26–10. The only game we won was the last, against Northland at Whangarei, 42–12, where I played right centre. It was a good experience for all of us and put me in good stead for the internationals against the Kiwis the following autumn. The hospitality was brilliant during our visit. Interestingly enough, Andy Platt and Neil Holding stayed 'Down Under' afterwards to play for the Brisbane Norths club. Once again, it was valuable experience for them. Our squad was a little bit older and wiser and we looked to build on our two-trophy success over the next 12 months.

9. Pride of the Lions

"Another accolade is that most coaches in our game always remind their players, before competing against Saints, to 'stop Pinner'. That alone is success."
Maurice Bamford

As captain of St Helens, things were generally going well. The team had broken its trophy drought and I was happy with my own form. I felt as though an international call-up against the Kiwis was a distinct possibility in the autumn of 1985. What I did want to do was to make up for the bad luck I had encountered in the summer of 1984, when things didn't quite go according to plan in Australia.

As it happened, I was delighted to be named in the initial training squad and part of the international set-up for the first time in several years. There were new people in charge of the Great Britain set-up and it certainly seemed as though the RFL really meant to improve the status of our international challenge. Something needed to be done. Great Britain were very much third in the pecking order behind Australia and the Kiwis. At the very least, we needed to match the New Zealanders in a three-match series to give us the confidence against the Australians, who were the real kingpins.

I had come across the New Zealanders before, of course. I had played two tests against the Kiwis in 1980 on their last tour and the series was drawn. The New Zealanders had a relatively young team then, which had matured a lot in four years. In fact, some of their players had been in demand from both English and Australian clubs. Hull signed three – James Leuluai, Gary Kemble and Dane O'Hara – and names like Mark Graham, Mark Broadbent and Gordon Smith were well known to English crowds. They were powerful opponents and the RFL had appointed a new management team to get the right results.

Maurice Bamford was the new coach, who had no experience of international rugby league as such, but had been in charge of clubs like Leeds and Wigan at top level. Unlike Frank Myler before him, he had no club connections and Great Britain was his only focus. Maurice was an extremely passionate man who wanted only the best for the Great Britain squad. His assistant was Phil Larder, who was director of coaching at the RFL, with Les Bettinson as team manager. Mike Stabler, who had been at Saints for a spell was the designated physio and Doctor Milton Novis was also on hand for further medical assistance. Maurice also brought in Dave Allred, the famous kicking coach, who took several 'tutorial' sessions with our kickers.

The main objective for the 1985 series was to try and improve the physical conditioning, preparation and performance on a par with the Australians. Maurice went over to see the trans-Tasman tests, won 2–1 by Australia, and came back determined to make us the best-prepared international squad in the history of Great Britain test matches.

Things were certainly different. We had a special camp at Lilleshall in Shropshire, where the squad of 30 would split into three teams of 10. There were some fun days, but one day planned for fun activities. There was a press day planned, and we did all our skill drills – handling, kicking and tackling ... but as we warmed up we got notice that the press corps bus had broken down and they would not be coming. Bamford had decided that the next day would be a fun day: sack races, egg and spoon races, wheelbarrow races and throwing the cricket ball. It was decided to do them since the press lads were not coming. Les Bettinson's face turned pale as he saw the press boys, about a dozen, who had arrived after all just in time to see Tony Myler winning the egg and spoon race. Then a concert in the evening – each team did their own thing.

On a personal note, one thing to come out of the bonding week was my appointment as captain for the series, which was a tremendous source of pride. The general feeling was that Maurice couldn't really make up his mind between the possible candidates. Andy Goodway and Ellery Hanley had been used, but he wasn't really satisfied with them. We went to the lecture theatre at Lilleshall and filled in a special questionnaire. One of the questions was 'Which player do you respect or admire the most?' Apparently the unanimous choice was – Harry Pinner. I didn't need much motivation after that.

During the week of a test, Monday to Friday, we would stay at a golfing hotel at Shaw Hill in Chorley, which certainly made us feel as though our preparation was being taken seriously. We started to use video analysis and our strengths would be highlighted by Larder, together with a full breakdown of our opponents. This included their angles of running; kicking game and, most importantly, who to run at. It seemed as though everything possible was provided to help us in our quest to win the series and to put British rugby league on the map once again. For once, the preparation could not be faulted.

We also had a mascot, a lion called *Sully* after the late, great Clive Sullivan who had passed away shortly before. There's no doubt that Maurice was a strict disciplinarian and made sure we really knuckled down in training. He was certainly never afraid to give us a real rollocking if he thought our standards were slipping in any way. As a coach, he put in his own ideas and moves, but was never afraid of us trying our own things during a game if need be.

The two squads were packed with quality players and the Brits were really determined to come away with a series win. Our last line of defence was Mick Burke, from Widnes, a St Helens lad, who was a powerful player; good under pressure and although he lacked genuine pace, he had a good rugby brain. He had the ability to force an opponent towards the touchline side before tackling him. On the right wing was Des Drummond, a really powerful guy, who had an unusual head-down running style. He wasn't a big man as such, but tremendously strong and a nightmare to tackle. I remember playing against Warrington one day and I told Neil Holding to avoid kicking to him at all costs. One kick went straight to him and he came through and smashed his way into our line.

Unfortunately, the first point of contact was yours truly. He hit me in the ribs with his head and it felt like they had come out of my back. The pain was terrible. At centre was Garry Schofield, who played with a strong Hull side. Despite some success at club level, he certainly found fame at international level in particular. He became one of the stars of the series with his pace and finishing ability – A complete footballer in many ways.

Ellery Hanley also played in the centre and what a player. Supreme upper-body strength, coupled with the ability to evade tacklers made him a formidable opponent. Ellery was good then, but he would be perfect in the modern-day game, with its – sometimes over – emphasis on strength and power. Wigan's Joe Lydon had pace and was an intelligent player, playing in a team that was starting to dominate the First Division. Joe could play anywhere in the backs with confidence and he became a good friend when we met up for the internationals. So too did Tony Myler – a brilliant stand-off, with great pace, as good as anyone in that position I have ever played with or against, which, I suppose, given some Australian number sixes, is quite a compliment in itself.

Deryck Fox, from Featherstone, didn't quite have Tony's pace, but he was a fine player at international level and did what he needed to do very effectively indeed. He topped the tackle count in the second test, ahead of some notable players. We could also bring in Shaun Edwards for either the full-back or half-back roles, who was, of course, by now a highly-experienced player after many games with Wigan.

As for the pack, Lee Crooks had been standing up to superior opponents since his introduction in the 1982 series against the Kangaroos. He never took a backward step and was a deceptively good footballer too, as well as an accomplished goalkicker. Jeff Grayshon, the old war-horse, then playing for Leeds was a shock selection by Maurice Bamford and played in the last two tests. At almost 37 years of age, he proved to be still worth a place at international level. A good scrummager, with a fantastic work-rate, he was a vital member of our pack, especially when the going got tough.

John Fieldhouse was one of the other front-rowers, who ran and tackled all day. He was physically fit and would have been a good addition to the Saints pack during the 1984–85 season, although the club ended up swapping me for him when I went to Widnes some time later.

At hooker was David Watkinson. Very much an old-school hard-knock number nine who had no prejudice whatsoever. He didn't mind who he belted. I would rather play with than against him and like any good hooker in those days, he could win his fair share of possession. The back-row initially had running power, in the shape of Andy Goodway and tackling power, with Ian Potter, both from Wigan, although Ian was another St Helens lad who had slipped through the net. Potter was one of the most formidable tacklers in the game in the sense that he would go low and scythe players down. Perhaps he needed lads to come in and smother the ball, but he did his job well. Maybe he was too clinical at times and was less intimidating than lads like Alan Rathbone and Tony Cotterrill, who would come in much higher with the idea of causing much physical pain. But a great player nevertheless.

Those who also played included David Hulme from Widnes, who was hard and aggressive, despite his size, and could cover in the halves. My Saints team-mate Chris Arkwright was of the same mould and could cover at centre and back row. His strength was a huge asset, but he was a great footballer and proved it with his performance at stand-off during the 1985 Premiership Final against Hull KR.

Chris Burton added aggression and power from the bench in the second test: another who didn't take a backward step. The Beardmore twins, Bob and Kevin also made up the squad and would certainly not have let anyone down. Kevin was probably more of a 'footballing' hooker than Dave Watkinson, but Dave had that intimidating factor.

We were up against powerful opponents who had a good mixture of power and rugby ability, what would be expected from a Kiwi side in fact. They tried James Leuluai at full-back at first, but he was really a half-back with a deceptive side-step, quite pacey and difficult to tackle. Dean Bell began the series on the wing, but he was more at home at centre and was a fiery character, as I remembered from that dust-up with Chris Arkwright when he played for Carlisle.

Fred Ah Kuoi was a constructive centre and was joined by Gary Prohm for the first test. Prohm was powerful, built like John Joyner in a way and played at loose-forward in the final test, when their team was reshuffled to try and get the series victory. Dane O'Hara was on the other wing, who had pace and was a really good finisher. Gary Kemble was also a fine full-back, tall, quite rangy and very difficult to tackle when he ran the ball out.

One of the surprises of the tour was the inclusion of a giant stand-off from Eastern Suburbs in Australia called Olsen Philipaina. He seemed to be a bit lumbering at first sight, but although he was one big unit, he needed some stopping.

At scrum-half was a real pest. Clayton Friend was ideally suited to test match rugby with his never-say-die attitude and good football brain. He was a typical scrum-half of the time, but a very good one.

The forwards were very strong. Kurt Sorenson and his brother Dane, who played together at Cronulla in Australia, formed a formidable front-row. Kurt, especially, would go toe-to-toe with anyone and normally came out on top. Dane was in the same mould and could kick goals, with hooker Howie Tamati very much a sort of modern-day acting half-back, with a very clean delivery to his first receiver.

Kevin Tamati, then of Warrington, was another hard man. I don't necessarily think he was what would be called a 'dirty' player, but he was really solid and probably in my top five players as far as toughness was concerned. Their back row was strong to say the least. Captain Mark Graham was a truly great player, who had the lot. He was strong, could run and had excellent hands. They had another lad called Owen Wright who played back-row who was tough, but not in the same way as the likes of Tamati. In fact, we knew quite a bit of what to expect from the Kiwis, with a number of them playing in the UK: Ah Kuoi, Kemble, Leuluai and O'Hara played for Hull; Gary Prohm for Hull KR and Kevin Tamati was at Warrington, with Wigan's captain Graeme West also in the squad. So the scene was set for a really competitive series and we all were fully concentrating on beating the 'Men in Black'.

Off on the wrong foot

There was one distraction for me, however. The week before the first test, it appeared that Leigh had approached Saints to see if I was available for transfer. It was a bit of a shock to be the target for a Second Division club, when I was enjoying my testimonial year and was captain of club and country. Saints' chairman Lawrie Prescott came out with the usual disclaimer about me not being available at any price. Alex Murphy was the Leigh coach and confirmed the approach was a serious one. He reckoned every player had a price and quoted the example of my Great Britain team-mate Ellery Hanley, who had left Bradford Northern for Wigan in a big-money deal.

Although we were pretty confident about getting off to a winning start, it was never going to be easy, as we found to our cost. But we got off to a flyer and our plan to expose Leuluai at full-back paid off when he spilled one of my high kicks and Andy Goodway scored the first try very early in the game, which Mick Burke converted. They brought regular full-back Kemble on as a substitute at half-time and this certainly improved the balance of their team. About five minutes after our try, Dane O'Hara scored for them, although it was not converted. Then we lost the plot a little. Dean Bell scored, closely followed by Mark Graham, who was really having a blinder. We also lost Lee Crooks. Filipaina converted the last one and we found ourselves 14–6 down. Just before half-time we got on the sheet again ourselves when Ellery powered his way over, with Burke kicking the goal and we went into the dressing room 14–12 down. Things could have been much worse.

Mick Burke equalised with a penalty goal just before the hour mark, but we never really seemed to take the game by the scruff of the neck when Mark Graham went off injured. Kurt Sorenson got a try shortly after the penalty goal – 18–14 – and Joe Lydon kicked a penalty to keep us in with a shout at 18–16 to the Kiwis.

Then came the moment we thought we had won it. It started with Des Drummond fielding a ball from near his own line. Chris Arkwright and Deryck Fox were involved before Hanley made a brilliant run down the touchline. It must have been over 50 yards and he ended up lobbing a pass to Joe Lydon who went over. He converted his own try and we had regained the lead, 22–18, after 72 minutes.

Five minutes later, came a disaster for us. Kurt Sorenson – who else – burst through and passed to Leuluai who went over by the posts. Filipaina converted, his second from five kicks, and they had stolen it from us. It must have been a really good game for the spekkies, but we were disappointed, to say the least; deflated in fact. The Kiwis had almost held the Australians in their last game and had lost in similar fashion, so we tried to look at the positives, after all we had matched them for most of the 80 minutes. It was no consolation whatsoever to be given the official Man-of-the-Match award for Great Britain, although I must have played well to prevent stand-off Tony Myler from getting it. He had a brilliant game. What a player he was at his best.

Test match number 232
Great Britain (12) 22 New Zealand (14) 24
19 October 1985
Headingley, Leeds.
Great Britain: Burke (Widnes, 3G), Drummond (Leigh), Schofield (Hull), Hanley (Wigan 1T), Lydon (Wigan, 1T 2G), Myler (Widnes), Fox (Bradford), Crooks (Hull), Watkinson (Hull KR), Fieldhouse (Widnes), Goodway (Wigan 1T), Potter (Wigan), Pinner (St Helens Capt) Subs: D. Hulme (Widnes), Arkwright (St Helens)
New Zealand: Leuluai (Hull, 1T), Bell (Easts Sydney, 1T), Ah Kuoi (Hull), Prohm (Hull KR), O'Hara (Hull, 1T), Filipaina (East Sydney, 2G), Friend (Auckland (Auckland), K Sorenson (Cronulla 1T), Tamati (Taranaki), D Sorenson (Cronulla), Graham (Norths Sydney Capt, 1T), Wright (Auckland), McGahan (Easts Sydney). Subs: Kemble (Hull), Tamati (Warrington)
Referee: B Gomersall (Australia)
Attendance: 12,591

Next stop was Central Park. Quite simply this was the one we just had to win to resurrect hopes of a series victory. I remember going over to the crowd with Jeff Grayshon and parading the Union Jack. Maurice was a great patriot and made sure we were the same, otherwise we wouldn't have worn the jersey. From that point I think the crowd were really with us from the off. We knew that, despite New Zealand losing Mark Graham just before the game to an ankle injury, we still had to improve our defence and this was part of Maurice Bamford's team talk. We knew we could score tries and our midfield triangle of me, Myler and Hanley could spark our attack into life. We just went for it from the start and, fortunately, it paid off.

It was typical test match stuff early on, with a penalty apiece from both sides. Then we started to cut loose. From a scrum, the ball went wide to Hanley, who sent Garry Schofield over for a try from 25 yards with a great inside pass. He had been around for a while, but he was still just 20 years old. He scored again on the half-hour and we were really in control at 12–2 when we went in at half-time.

Maurice told us to increase our intensity when we got back out and to imagine that we were losing. It wasn't long before we scored again and I can remember being involved in the early stages of the move before Myler put Schofield in for his third try from something like 50 yards. New Zealand replied with a try from Dean Bell, but they never looked like troubling us. I put a drop-goal over to make sure and made a break that led to Garry Schofield getting his fourth try. This equalled the British test match record and a new points record against New Zealand. The crowd went mad after that and in the dressing room afterwards there was champagne everywhere and a few tears were shed I'm not ashamed to say. Happy days indeed and we looked forward to the final test at Elland Road.

Test match number 233

Great Britain (12) 25 New Zealand (2) 8
2 November 1985
Central Park, Wigan.
Great Britain: Burke (Widnes), Drummond (Leigh), Schofield (Hull, 4T), Hanley (Wigan), Lydon (Wigan, 4G), Myler (Widnes), Fox (Featherstone Rovers), Crooks (Hull), Watkinson (Hull KR), Fieldhouse (Widnes), Goodway (Wigan 1T), Potter (Wigan), Pinner (St Helens Capt, DG) Subs: Edwards (Wigan), Burton (Hull KR)
New Zealand: Kemble (Hull), Bell (Easts Sydney, 1T), Leuluai (Hull), Prohm (Hull KR), O'Hara (Hull), Fillipaina (Easts Sydney Capt, 2G), Friend (Auckland (Auckland), K Sorenson (Cronulla, 1T), Tamati (Taranaki), D Sorenson (Cronulla), West (Wigan), Stewart (Wellington), McGahan (Easts Sydney). Subs: Ah Kuoi (Hull), Cowan (Auckland)
Referee: B. Gomersall (Australia)
Attendance: 15,506

91

Great Britain 22 New Zealand 24
Looking to off-load, despite the attentions of Hugh McGahan.
Dave Watkinson and Ian Potter are behind Harry. (Courtesy Alex Service)

Great Britain 25 New Zealand 8. Flying the flag, with Jeff Grayshon, before the
crucial second test at Wigan. It really got the crowd going.
(Courtesy *Rugby League Journal*)

Great Britain 25 New Zealand 8. Interview at pitch side, with Ellery Hanley and some fans. (Courtesy *Rugby League Journal*)

Great Britain 6 New Zealand 6. On the break at Elland Road in the test decider. Kiwi captain Mark Graham and Great Britain's Derryck Fox are in the background. (Courtesy *Rugby League Journal*)

A series win – and vital World Cup points – was on the cards for us, but we knew the match was going to be a physical one. I remember getting a gash above my eye after my first tackle and thinking how tough test match rugby was. However, it was going to get much tougher than I thought. After about 15 minutes, Andy Goodway was stretchered off after an off-the-ball tackle from Kurt Sorenson and that was his afternoon over. He was sent to the sin-bin for five minutes. Did the punishment fit the crime? Ridiculous! The Kiwis certainly were starting to cut up rough, but Goodway's exit brought on Lee Crooks, who went on to have a brilliant game. The feeling was that the referee, Barry Gomersall from Australia, was rather lenient and tended to let the game flow and let both sides hammer each other rather than clamp down on foul play.

On the half-hour, our defence was broken as Mark Graham, their Man-of-the-Match, went over from a play-the-ball, Dane Sorenson kicked the goal and that score remained until the break. It was a bad try to concede. The lads did say that he didn't get the ball down, but later on Gomersall said that it would have been a try anyway, because John Fieldhouse had interfered at the ruck and he would have given a penalty try. We certainly missed Tony Myler at stand-off, although Maurice moved Hanley to number six and Shaun Edwards came in at centre.

In the third quarter, Lee Crooks banged over two penalties to reduce the deficit to just two points. As I said, it was a rough, tough game and it looked like things were about to boil over at any time. In the 63rd minute it did. An all-out brawl erupted from a scrum. It seemed to carry on for quite some time and when Gomersall intervened, he sent Grayshon and Kurt Sorenson to the sin bin for 10 minutes. But he had a bit of help and it wasn't just the touch judges. Two police officers came onto the field because they thought that the brawl had lasted too long and things were getting out of hand.

New Zealand had a change at hooker and they brought in Wayne Wallace, who was like an 'angry ant' and he had a go at Watkinson, who ended up with a nasty eye gash. This was one of those brutal test matches and there was no question that the Kiwis wanted to disrupt our attacking flow. Apparently the penalty count, 20–7 to us, reflected the physical nature of the match, but with so many penalties in our favour, we were perhaps disappointed not to have won the game by a reasonable margin.

Then our last chance of salvaging the series came just before the hooter. Gomersall gave us a penalty 30 yards out on the Best Stand side. There was only one option. I told Lee Crooks to have a go and he produced one of the great 'pressure kicks' of test match rugby to draw the match and the series. In fact, as he was teeing up the ball, they were announcing he was the Man-of-the-Match, so whether he heard that or not, I don't know, but it would have given him a real boost. Apparently,

Honours even. Harry sharing the Whitbread trophy with Mark Graham – a great player and fearsome opponent. (Courtesy *Rugby League Journal*)

Maurice Bamford couldn't bear to look. To be fair, the Kiwis had tackled well and we rarely looked like getting over their line, so it was a fair result in some ways.

Test match number 234 (World Cup rated)
Great Britain (0) 6 New Zealand (6) 6
9 November 1985
Elland Road, Leeds.
Great Britain: Burke (Widnes); Drummond (Leigh), Schofield (Hull), Edwards (Wigan), Lydon (Wigan); Hanley (Wigan), Fox (Featherstone Rovers); Grayshon (Leeds), Watkinson (Hull KR), Fieldhouse (Widnes), Goodway (Wigan), Potter (Wigan), Pinner (St Helens Capt) Subs: Arkwright (St Helens), Crooks (Hull 3G)
New Zealand: Kemble (Hull); Williams (Auckland), Bell (Easts Sydney), Leuluai (Hull), O'Hara (Hull 1T); Ah Kuoi (Hull), Friend (Auckland); Tamati (Warrington), Wallace (Canterbury), D Sorenson (Cronulla 1G), Graham (Norths Sydney Capt 1T), K Sorenson (Cronulla), Prohm (Hull KR). Subs: Filipaina (Easts Sydney), McGahan (Easts Sydney)
Referee: B Gomersall (Australia)
Attendance: 22,209

The series was a great success for rugby league in this country. We had won back our self-esteem and won over the supporters after such a long spell when it seemed as though we could only compete against the French – and they were arguably in decline. The squad, in my opinion,

95

had the best threequarter line in the world. Des Drummond and Joe Lydon were really class acts on the wings and in Hanley and Schofield, we had two more who were now world class. In the halves, Deryck Fox and Tony Myler were forming a brilliant partnership and our overall discipline had improved such a lot from previous years, despite potential provocation and some not-too-strict refereeing.

Perhaps one of the most flattering articles in my scrapbook is from Maurice Bamford himself, who was talking to the *St Helens Star*. Given the fact that I had taken over the captaincy of the team with relatively little experience, his comments made me feel very good indeed: "I couldn't have had a better man leading my team. He was the players' choice and it proved a popular decision. The lad gave his all for Great Britain and after working with him I appreciate his commitment. It's foolish to knock him, because he has so much flair. He lifted the lads and took the game to New Zealand. The matches brought out the best in people and Harry Pinner is the most complete leader I have ever selected … I was proud of with the results but also delighted for Harry because I know how much leading the national team meant to him. He was superb and a fine ambassador for rugby league both on and off the field."

In those days it wasn't a case of resting on your laurels. I remember the following day after the last test playing for Saints against Dewsbury at Knowsley Road in the first round of the John Player Special Trophy. Although I was stiff and aching, I seemed to have a good game and we won relatively easily. We combined well as a team and our two Australian signings, Brett French and Ross Conlon scored tries. I asked Ellery Hanley where he was going to the day after one test and he said he wasn't really looking forward to going to the Zoo. This wasn't in Chester – he was going to Wilderspool Stadium in Warrington, which was an intimidating place to go at the time. Playing two games in two days would not happen in the modern game. The Easter fixtures, Good Friday and Easter Monday, have been subject to review by the RFL, with the idea of reducing it to one. Given the size and power of today's players, I can see where the idea is coming from.

10. Bitter sweet

"As a player he sometimes makes it look easy because he is such a good reader of the game, and has a good positional sense to match. He is there in the right place at the right time, he has a wonderful pair of hands and as a ball distributor he has no peers."
Vince Karalius

Shocks to the system

The achievements with the Saints in 1984–85 and drawing the test series against the Kiwis the following year were certainly up there with anything I could ever have wished for. On the international front there was another huge challenge on the horizon, with the Kangaroos arriving at the start of the 1986–87 season. Needless to say, I wanted to be a part of it and for Great Britain to build on what we did against the Kiwis, even though it would be up another level. The important thing was to maintain my club form and just see how things developed.

It's a great shame that Mal Meninga could never come back for another spell with us, as he was such a huge favourite and gave us a big advantage out wide. Full-back Phil Veivers did stay at Knowsley Road, however, and the younger lads who had come through the ranks, like Paul Round and Andy Platt were now regular first teamers, and, in the case of Platt, knocking on the representative door.

1985–86 was going to be a crucial season for us all. The fans had tasted success after our lean spell and, naturally, wanted more. It put pressure on the club and, of course, who could possibly replace Mal Meninga? Two Australians were signed during the close season: Ross Conlon, from Balmain – an Australian international centre or winger who was a specialist goalkicker – and Brett French from Wynnum Manly, who was a centre with some pace to burn. But it was hard for them at times ... the crowd really wanted Mal, of course. Later in the season we signed the big Kiwi centre Mark Elia, who strengthened the back line with his powerful running.

We began the season against Swinton, at Bolton FC's Burnden Park, and looked to be finding form early with a 32–14 victory. We progressed through to the Lancashire Cup semi-final and as the holders of the trophy, we thought that we would give Wigan a tough game, even though it was at Central Park. We had come off a home defeat by Hull and it is fair to say that confidence was not too high. In the end we were blown away by 30–2, in front of a crowd of 18,544. The following week, Castleford turned us over at Wheldon Road 32–18. We beat Hull KR at Knowsley Road quite comfortably on 20 October, but seven days later came another shock to system, with the visit of the Kiwis to Knowsley Road. As two-trophy winners from the previous season, we were expected to give them a really hard match and the game was broadcast live in New Zealand. Unfortunately, we were blown away 46–6 and it proved to be the end for our coach Billy Benyon, who was sacked on Monday 18 November. We had actually lost five out of seven matches including the Kiwi debacle, so maybe the writing was on the wall. I had only played in two of those seven games because of injury, with Chris Arkwright taking over the loose forward role. The club said that results and, of course, falling attendances had become a real worry and they were envious of what Wigan were able to do by bringing a number of world class stars to Central Park, such as my Great Britain team-mates Ellery Hanley and Andy Goodway, plus Australians like Steve Ella.

There was even one train of thought that said that Alex Murphy, who was, after all, a larger than life character, could help to make up for the loss of Mal Meninga. The Saints Alive Society was formed to help raise cash for team-building, which was certainly a positive step.

It was still a shock for everyone in the team when Billy Benyon got the sack. There was a good bond established between coach and players and, I suppose, it was an uncertain time with a new face coming to the club. Our chairman, Lawrie Prescott, later unveiled Alex Murphy as the new coach, or rather, 'the return of the Messiah'. I didn't necessarily feel uncertain at this point. After all, Murphy had always seemed to value me as a player and, no matter which club he was at, he made a bid for my transfer. So in that sense, it seemed all right. Unfortunately, it became a bit of a nightmare for me.

He would come into the dressing room at about 2.45pm and tried to fire the lads up, highlighting the weaknesses in the opposition. If we were playing, say, Widnes, it would be 'get into that Tony Myler and make sure he doesn't dominate the game'. The trouble is, I knew what was coming after a few matches and it just went over my head. I really rated Alex as a player – my dad said he was the greatest English player he had ever seen – and as a player-coach, but not in the same way as a coach. I just found that what I saw as his 'rule by fear' and confrontational style approach was not for me. Don't get me wrong, it worked for some of the lads, but not for me and I should say straight away that I was no 'Peter Perfect' myself on occasions too, if I didn't agree on something. I spoke my mind. Maybe that didn't help either.

I suppose Alex saw me not just as captain, but as a sort of shop steward for the lads and, I think, was quite wary of me. I remember going in once to ask him what bonus we were on for a match at Leeds and he went mad. I said the lads wanted to know and it was a big incentive for them, but he wouldn't tell me. There always seemed to be a barrier between us and it continued until I left the club.

Mixed emotions

The 1985–86 campaign really became one of contrasts. I was leading the Great Britain team to a tied test series against the Kiwis and experiencing some marvellous elation at that level of rugby, whereas on the domestic front, I wasn't enjoying myself to anything like the same extent. After the Saints versus New Zealand match, however, we won at Featherstone and were unbeaten in our next eight games, ending with a 22–4 defeat against Hull KR in the semi-final of the John Player Special Trophy at Headingley.

I missed the match through injury and didn't play in the next five games, which were all lost. Andy Platt, Chris Arkwright and Shaun Allen wore the 13 jersey in my absence. I returned against Featherstone Rovers at Knowsley Road on 2 February and we hammered them 44–14. Probably no coincidence, but you never know. I was able to play against Dewsbury in the Challenge Cup First Round at Leeds, with their undersoil heating enabling the game to be played. Dewsbury's own pitch was frozen solid. We won 22–19. In the next round, we drew Wigan away and lost 24–14, after being 10–4 up at half-time, which was a real choker. The spekkies really hated any defeat against the old enemy, but there was something positive to cheer afterwards.

From that point the team remained un-beaten in the league until the end of the season and finished in third place, a point behind Wigan and just two behind Halifax, who were Slalom Lager Champions with 44 points. We had 42. What a pity we couldn't have got those three points at some stage during the year. Considering all the turmoil during the season, especially before the New Year, this was a creditable effort from the players, although they lost at home against sixth-placed Leeds in the first round of the Premiership. I was injured again and Chris Arkwright wore the number 13 in that game. The crowd for that match was just 6,415 and it seemed that despite the improvement, it was still a difficult task to get the fans on the terraces.

I was also in my testimonial year with Saints and we had a committee whose task it was to organise various events. For the record they were: Jimmy O'Sullivan (Chairman), George Connolly (Vice-Chairman), Cliff Middlehurst (Treasurer), Geoff Cropper (Secretary), Graham Holland, Walter Cunningham, Margaret Burrows, Chris Platt, Janet Davies, Enid Parsons, Miriam Birchall, Lennie Lowe, Keith Highcock and Dave Parr.

I will never forget the work they put in on my behalf. Geoff Cropper, in particular, felt that I had been short-changed in terms of getting a car from the club. He saw that some of the overseas players were getting sponsored cars and there was me, captain of Great Britain, driving around in my beaten-up Sirrocco.

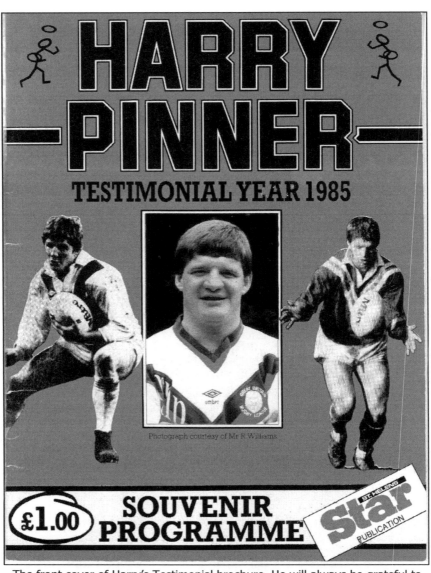

The front cover of Harry's Testimonial brochure. He will always be grateful to those who made the year so successful. (Courtesy Alex Service)

St. Helens 42 Dewsbury 6, John Player Trophy. Saints line up.
Back row: Eric Leach (Kit), Shaun Allen, Graham Liptrot, Brett French,
Tony Burke, Peter Gorley, Phil Veivers, Chris Arkwright, Gary Greinke (Sub),
Alex Murphy (Coach); Front row: Roy Haggerty, Neil Holding, Andy Plattt,
Barry Ledger, Harry Pinner (Capt), Kevin Meadows, Steve Peters (Sub).
(Courtesy Alex Service)

St Helens 42 Dewsbury 6, John Player Trophy
Leading out the team in full glare of the cameras,
with new coach Alex Murphy pointing the way.
(Courtesy Alex Service)

Geoff went to Broughton's garage in Knowsley Road and talked to a guy called Graham Smedley who came up with a white Citroen with a red vee on the front. Now that was class.

The real down-side to my testimonial year was the fact that I made just 19 full appearances in the 1985–86 campaign. Naturally it did have an impact on the testimonial itself. Five players made over 30 appearances: Barry Ledger (37), Chris Arkwright (35), Roy Haggerty (33), Neil Holding (33) and Phil Veivers (30). One new face who was quite battle-hardened gave the team much-needed experience – Eric Hughes was signed from Widnes, who was usually a centre but played stand-off with great effect.

Later, Kevin McCormack began challenging for a place on the wing and Paul Loughlin finished the season at left centre, which was his best position. There was cover for Graham Liptrot, with Dave Harrison proving a capable reserve.

My last match of the season, as it happened, was on Good Friday against Wigan at Knowsley Road. We beat them 18–13, but things went against me. This was my testimonial match and on the morning of the game, the club put me on the transfer list. It was not a particularly good piece of timing, to say the least, and potentially quite damaging – in fact disastrous – to the match-day collection that was going to happen.

Perhaps after that particular kick in the guts it was time for a reappraisal of my position at Knowsley Road.

The end is nigh

The 1986–87 season was a truly a disaster for me at Saints. I just couldn't get fit and was plagued by knee ligament and ankle trouble. I endured a daily visit to Manchester to have special exercises and physiotherapy, but it was a long while before I regained anything like full fitness. The spekkies were, perhaps, getting a little restless. 'Where's Pinner again? What's up with him?' I played in our second league match at Salford, which we won 38–4, but I missed out on a vital Lancashire Cup semi-final at Wigan, when the floodlights failed for a spell, and looked to get fit for the visit of the Australian tourists in early November.

Given the nature of my bad start, I was not initially considered for the Great Britain squad and David Watkinson took over the captaincy for the forthcoming test match series, which I desperately wanted to play in.

I managed to put two games together at Barrow and at home to Salford, both of which we won, but little did I realise it, but that would be my last game in the Red Vee of St Helens. The team went on to lose 32–8 to the Australians – Chris Arkwright was loose forward – and I honestly thought my chances of selection for the remainder of the series had all but disappeared. Just for the record, here is the last time I lined up with the Saints. It could have been worse, but on 17 October 1986, we beat Salford 32–14. For me, truly the end of an era: Veivers, Ledger (1T), Loughlin (8G), Halliwell, McCormack (1T), Clark (1T), Holding, Jarvis, Harrison, Burke, Platt (1T), Haggerty, Pinner (Capt) Subs: Allen, Round

Saints perhaps realised that the end was going to come and put me on the transfer list for £95,000. Needless to say I thought this fee was ridiculous, although I could not see any way forward while Alex Murphy was coach. At one stage there was talk of a swap deal with Leigh for Des Drummond, but I didn't really want to go to a club that was struggling at the time.

The *St Helens Reporter* carried a story with the headline: 'Why I quit'. I was quoted as saying: "I've had enough. I'm not going to play for Saints any more. I do not think it right for me under the present circumstances. As far as I'm concerned I have retired. They have messed me about too much and when things are not right it is no use carrying on."

My last test match as captain for Great Britain was in Avignon on 16 February 1986. We were 2–0 down early on, but we fought back with two penalties from Lee Crooks to lead 4–2. A converted try from Ellery Hanley made the score 10–2 at half-time. But in the second half, French full-back Gilles Dumas scored a try on 46 minutes, converted it and then kicked a penalty on 62 minutes to make the score 10–10. I was the only St Helens player in the team.

France 10 Great Britain 10, Avignon 16 February 1986. The last time Harry captained his country. Back: Steve Hampson (Wigan), Ian Potter (Wigan), Mick Burke (Widnes), Kevin Rayne (Leeds – reserve), Lee Crooks (Hull), Garry Schofield (Hull); middle: Phil Larder (assistant coach), Tony Myler, Neil James (Halifax), Shaun Wane (Wigan – reserve), Ellery Hanley (Wigan), John Fieldhouse (Warrington), Henderson Gill (Wigan), Mike Stabler (physio), Doctor; front: Deryck Fox (Featherstone Rovers), David Watkinson (Hull KR), Les Bettinson (Manager), Harry Pinner (captain), Maurice Bamford (coach), Des Drummond, Shaun Edwards. (Courtesy *Rugby League Journal*)

11. Pastures new

"The mystery is that Harry does not have a sack full of Great Britain caps commensurate with his undoubted skills. He has suffered injuries at the wrong time, and, perhaps, is one of those players whose most brilliant performances are reserved for his club. Certainly, on his day, there is no more constructive or inspiring loose forward in the game."
Keith Macklin

Despite feeling that I was about to retire and concentrate on my pub business, the *St Helens Reporter* did carry a little snippet that there might well be a light at the end of the tunnel for me that might make me change my mind. There was still a possibility that a deal could be struck with Widnes for a straight swap with John Fieldhouse, the 24-year-old international second-rower. Murphy claimed that it was now up to me to agree terms with Widnes, but things appeared to have fallen through and for a while it was stalemate.

Then things started to happen very quickly indeed. It was a Sunday morning, 2 November 1986; I got up at about 8.30am and went for a training run. I must have done a few miles and then put my spikes on for some sprints. When I got back home to the Victoria Inn, I got a phone call from my good friend Duggie Laughton, who was the coach at Widnes, who wanted to talk terms with me. I went round to his house straight away and became a Widnes player there and then. Widnes had a home game that day and Duggie wanted me to play. At two o'clock I was still at his house; I had to dash home and sort things out with the pub and arrived at Naughton Park 20 minutes before kick-off, before the game against Hull KR.

Unfortunately, Richie Ayres was originally meant to play loose forward and he had to take his jersey off and give it to me. Of course, he wasn't very happy about it, but I just told him that it was one of those things and that if he was patient, he would get his rewards in the future. Although I was hardly match fit, I seemed to have a good game and was able to keep the ball moving. It was also great to link up with Tony Myler, who was a class act at stand-off. We must have moved the ball very well indeed, as our winger John Basnett scored five tries in our 26–8 victory. It was good to play 80 minutes of rugby again and to have a real influence out there on the field. I really wanted to do the best for Duggie, who I had great respect for and the Widnes club. It was a whole new challenge for me and I was determined to make the most of it.

Quite early on I had my own 'international trial' match. The Australians were touring and looked even more formidable then they did in 1982. We were playing them at Naughton Park on 12 November. I had been out of the reckoning with my injury problems, but I got a phone call from Maurice Bamford, who was going to watch my progress closely. If I did well, I would be back in the Great Britain side for the third test at Central Park. Now, we had lost the other two, but it was a chance for Maurice to get me back with scrum-half Andy Gregory and give the team a different dimension.

The Australians seemed to sense that a test match place was up for grabs for me and they absolutely pummelled me. I could hardly get out of bed the following day. In one incident, their forwards held me up and one of their half-backs came in and gave me an almighty belt. I got my own back later by stamping on his hand. I'm certainly not proud of doing that, but that's the way it was in those days.

Mal Meninga played at centre and they had some big forwards playing, including Paul Sironen, Les Davidson and Martin Bella, so they really meant business. I thought I had done enough to prove that I was worth a recall, but in truth it was one of the toughest 80 minutes of rugby league I had ever experienced at any level. Duggie Laughton was amazed that I'd taken so much 'stick' and stayed on the field for the 80 minutes. It wasn't all one-way and we tried to give as good as we got. Their back-rower Steve Folkes went off with a fractured cheekbone and the score at half-time was 8–2. We eventually lost 20–4, which was a big disappointment for the 10,268 crowd and I sensed that my team-mates had not really expected a match of such ferocity. However, I had passed my 'trial' and looked forward to renewing acquaintances with the Green and Golds in 10 days time

For the test match against the Australians at Wigan's Central Park, I was going through my usual pre-match routine whereby I wanted to retch. There was just the one big bath for the players, like at Knowsley Road and communal toilets. So I was trying to settle my nerves and some of the Australians were in there as well, including Meninga. He didn't speak, initially, while his team-mates were there, but when they had gone, he leaned over: "Harry, guess what, Debbie's just had a baby last night. We'll have to celebrate it after the game." Mal couldn't have shown friendship with the enemy with the likes of Lewis and Boyd there, but it was typical of him to let me know.

Anyhow when Maurice Bamford picked the team, he put Chris Burton in the second row. We knew that the Australian management had selected Mal Meninga in their back row. Before we kicked off I told Andy Gregory to kick it straight to Mal. Burton got into him straight away with his elbow and Mal didn't like it one bit. "Who's that dirty bastard who elbowed me, I couldn't remember the first half at all", he said later. I did feel a bit guilty that I was perhaps the one who had thought up the ploy in the first place. The Australians won 24–15, which was the closest score of the three test matches.

106

There were some great players at Widnes. The Hulme brothers were local products and hard as nails; Kurt Sorenson led by example up front, with Mike and Steve O'Neill. At full-back was Mick Burke, who had gone on the 1984 tour with me; Phil McKenzie was a lively hooker, with Darren Wright a powerful centre. They brought in Dale (Rowdy) Shearer from Australia and I remember putting him into a gap and he sailed away for a long-distance try.

And later there was a guy called Offiah who could shift a bit too. Despite some great players on the staff, we finished in eighth place in the First Division – a big disappointment. Our biggest chance for honours was in the Challenge Cup. We won 24–16 at Castleford in the first round; and drew with Bradford Northern at Odsal in the next round, before beating them 29–12 at home.

We then went to Leeds and won 14–7; we lost 35–6 at Headingley in the league six weeks before. So we had reached the semi-final, where we faced Halifax, also at Leeds. For us, it was a chance for an eighth Wembley visit in 12 years. It was a second home for Widnes in those days.

We were clear favourites, but in the cup, form goes out of the window. We found ourselves two tries down and struggling in the first half. I thought I had a better second-half and got the ball moving. We scored through Phil McKenzie with about 10 minutes to go, but they hung on and ended up beating St Helens at Wembley. So I was disappointed on two counts! What a game that would have been. As it was, we went to Knowsley Road in the league and won 30–24, which was some consolation, but failed to beat Wigan in the first round of the Premiership at Central Park – we lost 22–18 and I scored one of our tries – and our season was over.

The 1987–88 season saw Widnes well up there with the challengers for major honours, but it was a bad time for me, with a persistent shoulder injury constantly nagging away. I suppose that the large numbers of cortisone injections didn't help me in the long term. In fact, I still get bother with that left shoulder today. I managed just 11 matches. We lost in the Lancashire Cup semi-final to Wigan and were defeated by Saints at Knowsley Road in the John Player Special Trophy. Perhaps Widnes thought they needed to cut their losses with me. Reading the piece in the *Liverpool Echo* from that time embarrasses me a bit now, but the whole thing got me down. I was quite bitter at the time, too.

Clubs had always chased me and now I was being used to tempt other players away. Duggie Laughton had Richie Eyres and Paul Hulme coming through in the back row and he obviously thought he needed a prop more than a loose forward. So off to Leigh I went.

Pinner on move after outburst

"First Division leaders Widnes were involved in a dramatic double transfer today – just two minutes before the noon cup deadline. Former Great Britain skipper Harry Pinner stunned the club by asking for a transfer yesterday. Today Widnes responded by signing Derek Pyke from Leigh in return for Pinner plus £50,000. Pinner 31, played in yesterday's victory over Leigh, but surprised the club by storming: 'I'll never turn out for Widnes again.' Loose forward Pinner was linked with both Leigh and Swinton recently and added: 'I'm upset because I know nothing of these proposals. I'm finished at Widnes and won't play for them again after the way I have been treated.'"

Liverpool Echo, 11 January 1988

A Leyther boy

So I became a Leigh player and the main reason was that it was a chance to team up again with Billy Benyon. I suppose it is a bit like the modern-day footballers in the Premier League, but we had an agreement that should Leigh be relegated into the Second Division I could find another club. I was years ahead of my time, wasn't I? My former Saints team-mate Steve Peters was there too. My first game – I was also appointed captain – was against Swinton at Hilton Park and we won 22–16, although they came back strongly in the second half.

We did our very best to avoid the dreaded drop but there were other distractions, such as a first round Challenge Cup game against Saints at home. We lost 22–12, but it was interesting to look at the papers afterwards when they wrote about Alex Murphy's half-time team talk which basically said 'Stop Pinner and you'll stop Leigh.' For nearly an hour we played some good rugby. I remember putting the Kiwi lad, Jeff Clark into a gap and he passed to John Kerr, who scored a good try, but unfortunately my luck changed for the worst, as Martin Richards wrote in the *Daily Mirror:* "Harry Pinner's cup joy turned to despair in one fatal moment against his old club yesterday. Two immaculate passes from the new Leigh captain had carved out tries to give his side a 10–6 interval lead and put Saints on the rack. But after a try from Man of the Match Phil Veivers had given Saints a 16–12 lead, Pinner's imagination went too far seven minutes from time. A long speculative pass from the Great Britain skipper was intercepted by Saints' six feet two inches Kiwi centre Mark Elia, who raced in unopposed to the posts for the killer touchdown." It was a bitter pill to take, especially since I really wanted to get one over Saints and Murphy.

We stuck to our task in our relegation fight and kept going. Swinton and Hunslet were virtually already down and it was between us and Salford for that unwanted third-from-bottom third relegation slot.

108

Left: Harry as a Widnes player. He was determined to give it his best shot and was still the first-choice Great Britain captain.
(Courtesy Alex Service)

Middle: St Helens 23
Bradford Northern 16
28 August 1988.
Return of the Saint. Waiting to come on to the pitch, next to a Bradford Northern official.
(Courtesy Alex Service)

Left: Leading out the Carlisle team.
(Courtesy *Rugby League Journal*)

Unfortunately, against Bradford Northern, at Hilton Park, we lost quite heavily, 20–5 and I lost the plot somewhat. I belted their big – huge – front-rower Brendan Hill, a sort of death wish when I think about it and he came at me like the *Incredible Hulk*.

"You'll get it now, you gummy bastard," he said and, unfortunately the match developed into a huge all-out brawl. I remember looking over my shoulder in the bar afterwards, but nothing more came of it, thankfully. Perhaps not a good example for the captain to set.

Our next game was also at home and this time, thankfully, we really showed what we could do when we battered Warrington 25–8, who were desperate to get a top four spot – they eventually finished sixth. I managed to redeem himself and the cutting in my scrapbook says it all, really: "With skipper Harry Pinner welding Leigh's new-look pack into a tight and effective unit, Benyon's men dominated from first whistle to final hooter. Pinner displayed his full range of handling skills to supply the scoring pass for four of the tries, but it was prop Adrian Earner and second row pair Brian Dunn and Andy Collier who deserve the plaudits for their unflagging efforts in midfield." (*The Journal* 7 April 1988)

The relegation scrap went on to the last game of the season. We needed to beat Hull at Hilton Park so that we were level on points with Salford – and we had a superior points difference. Salford had to at least draw with Halifax to stay in the Championship. Both games were played at the same time. We beat Hull 31–9, but Salford won 36–16 to stay in the division. Their players earned £1,000 bonus per man – what might have been.

As I said, I did not want to play in the Second Division at this stage of my career and Billy Benyon understood my position. Oldham and Salford were interested, but I opted for Bradford and was offered a two-year contract, which I signed on 26 June 1988. Leigh was a very friendly club with a good atmosphere, but it didn't quite have the professionalism of Saints or Widnes and it was a shame things didn't work out. Ironically, I was voted the club's Player-of-the-Year too.

Running with Bradford Northern

I think the Bradford coach, Barry Seabourne thought I was the man to add skill to what was considered to be the most formidable pack in the British game. There was Brendan Hill, Brian Noble, Kelvin Skerrett and David Hamer up front with Karl Fairbank and David Hobbs in the second row. How about packing down behind that lot? It was probably as good a pack as any I played in. Apart from that, I knew quite a lot of the lads anyway. I was on tour with Brian Noble, Keith Mumby and David Hobbs in 1984 and I came across most of the others around the circuit. I was particularly looking forward to partnering scrum-half Paul Harkin, who I always rated as a player and I hoped that we would enjoy a partnership like Knocker Norton and Peter Sterling had at Hull. But there was to be a potentially awkward moment beforehand. We had a trip to the Isle of Man as part of what could be called a pre-season bonding exercise and they had me rooming with Brendan Hill. I found him to be a really good guy who – fortunately – didn't have any grudges. He was one big bear of a guy.

I really wanted to be successful at Odsal and in an article by Phil Thomas in the *Yorkshire Post* I was quoted as saying: "I'm really enjoying myself at Bradford and think I'll be here until I finish playing. I'd love to do well and win things for them after they saved me from the Second Division. As long as I keep enjoying myself then I'll carry on playing."

We did enjoy some success early on, although our first loss was at Knowsley Road in the opening game of the season. They actually beat us home and away and prevented us from getting seventh place in the Stones Bitter Championship table. We were two points behind, winning 11, losing 14 and drawing once. Our biggest achievement was getting to the John Player Special semi-final, where we lost 16–5 to Wigan at Headingley. Wigan beat us at Odsal in the second round of the Challenge Cup and went on to win it by nilling Saints at Wembley.

The forwards were the big strength of the team and Karl Fairbank (34), David Hobbs (32) and Brian Noble (34) made the most appearances. Steve McGowan, a long-striding centre, played 34 times, with full-back Keith Mumby 33. Those forwards were certainly not to be messed with. I can remember getting some 'treatment' from Widnes's Paul Moriarity and they took it in turns to smash him afterwards.

I was still capable of playing some good football and the *Daily Star's* Peter Wilson reported on one match, against Oldham, as follows:

Golden Oldie Pinner rips Oldham apart

"Harry Pinner, one-time Great Britain skipper now relegated to the subs' bench of Bradford sparked the revival that dumped Oldham closer to the second Division. The ex-St Helens and Widnes trick handling specialist came on when Northern – by no means free of relegation fears themselves – were trailing 14–12. But just one glimpse of the Pinner ball skills and it all changed. He sent Steve McGowan racing through a yawning gap and although the big-striding centre was held just short of the line, the damage was done. Karl Fairbank put the finishing touch and Northern were back in front … Super-sub Pinner played another important role in another Bradford try – McGowan's second – and in the last minute he was flattened by an off-the-ball incident that ended with Keith Newton being sent off. Newton looked suitably aggrieved, and with every reason. Referee Brian Simpson with the help of a touch judge had picked out the wrong man. Newton was all of 15 yards from the action." (23 January 1989)

Needless to say I can't remember who really flattened me, but I remember another quote in the press by Oldham coach Tony Barrow, who was a bit upset about their loss: "I will give 110 per cent but I can't vouch for the players. Tony Barrow is not Jesus Christ − I can't work miracles." He needed to. They were relegated with Halifax and Hull KR.

Unfortunately, the travelling was getting me down, although my dad, God bless him, did much to help by driving me up and down the M62, but I decided I'd had enough. I left Bradford on the best possible terms, albeit prematurely. I had an open mind about things and it looked like the end of my playing career had come and I thought about concentrating on pub life. How wrong could I be?

Cumbria Calling

In July 1989, I was approached by Second Division Carlisle and they signed me from Northern for £20,000. Given what I said about travelling to Yorkshire, it would probably seemed a strange decision on reflection. I did go there as a player and not as player-coach, Tommy Dawes was the coach, and made the move so that I could weigh up the Second Division as a whole and the requirements for a possible move into coaching. The Carlisle chairman was Alan Tucker, who ran Britax car seats, who was very enthusiastic about securing me as a player for the club. He wanted me to help realise the rugby potential of the area. My signing certainly grabbed the headlines, as this report by Phil Mason from the *Evening News and Star* suggests:

Ace Pinner for Carlisle

"Rugby league maestro Harry Pinner today signed for Carlisle from Bradford Northern. The former Great Britain skipper travelled to the city this afternoon and signed in a deal believed to be worth £40,000. It is a sensational coup by Carlisle and officials see his signature as the first step towards blasting out of the second division. Pinner's signature will not exactly be the last this summer. Pinner, one of the best ball-handling forwards and tacticians of the 1980s − was listed by Northern at £40,000." (Thursday 6 July 1989)

Perhaps, despite my best intentions, I knew deep down that the relationship was not going to be too long. I started driving up there in summer. No problem. But when the winter nights drew in it became too much. Two and a half hours on the road took its toll and I still had a business to run. Roy Lester, the former Fulham player and coach, who had coached the team before Tommy Dawes, was an area manager for a local brewery and there was talk about offering me a pub in the Lakes, if I was prepared to move up there as player-coach. My parents were in St Helens and I didn't want to be too far away from them and starting a business, almost from scratch, was a risky thing to do. In the end I saw no other option but to give it up.

Tommy Dawes was replaced by Cameron Bell, Dean's dad, in the New Year and the team finished fifth from bottom in the table, perhaps not where they expected to be given the early season hype.

The other side of the tracks

Obviously I thought that my rugby league involvement had ended there and then, so I was quite surprised to be phoned up by Jack Robinson, a Wigan director and he sounded me out about becoming John Monie's assistant at Central Park. I thought 'this is fantastic' and it was just a short distance from home. Ideal. I didn't mind giving up the playing side at all. My job spec was 'Coaching co-ordinator' and I took up the job after Jeff Hurst had resigned, when Graham Lowe, the previous coach, had resigned. Other members of the coaching set-up were Australian fitness expert Bob Lanigan, Bill Hartley, who was the sprint trainer and Graeme West (Alliance team boss) who I knew well from club and international matches.

This might sound a bit strange, but I found it hard, on occasions, to coach lads I had played with and roomed with on tours, such as Joe Lydon, Andy Gregory, Ellery Hanley and Shaun Edwards. In retrospect it would have been better to go to a club where I was not as familiar to the players.

I did help to get another of my former team-mates, Kelvin Skerrett, to Wigan from my links with Bradford and he proved to be a great signing for them. If they had brought over Karl Fairbank with him, they would have been invincible. Wigan had a tremendously talented group of players and the secret was to keep all of them happy and keep harmony in the group. There were some potentially big egos and personality clashes, although winning matches and trophies is a big advantage in that respect and Wigan were doing just that. I remember Shaun Edwards would even do his own 'video analysis' before John and I sat down to do the same on Monday mornings.

John Monie followed his predecessors with a raft of silverware: Challenge Cup, League titles, Regal Trophies and so on, but like I said, his man management had to be spot on to harness the talent at his disposal – and it was absolutely brilliant. He was a thinking man's coach, who never bawled and shouted in the hope of getting a response. The shouters and bawlers were not necessarily the answer and I don't think I even heard John swear.

He knew so much about the game and analysed things at a different level to anything I'd seen before. John was so precise in everything he did and was years ahead of his time. My stay at Central Park ended before Christmas in 1991. It was the end of an era for me. Anne and I had a new arrival, our daughter Joanne, plus the pressures of pub life. In the *Rugby Leaguer*, I explained my decision to quit: "I have never worked with a finer coach than John Monie. As far as I'm concerned he is 'The Master'. I have learned so much in the time I have been at Wigan and I am extremely grateful to John and the Wigan board for the opportunity to work at a club that I consider to be the most professionally run in the business. John Monie, the directors and the players have been terrific with me and it's with a certain element of regret that I have had to make my decision to leave. But I am the landlord of the Victoria pub in Newton-le-Willows, a demanding job in its own right. Something had to go and after nearly 20 years in the game, I decided it was time for a break. I intended leaving last season, but John persuaded me to stay on. Coaching at the top level takes up so much time and my family and livelihood are much more important to me."

People ask me if I had ever had any regrets during my rugby career and I tell them that I was so privileged to play and captain my local team and go on to do the same with my country. But if there was one major regret, it was not to continue with my coaching career. In retrospect, how good it would have been to have gone on to eventually coach a team like Saints. People like John Monie showed where coaching was heading and I regret not being a part of it once I left Central Park. But it was not to be and I naturally value the opportunities I had to play for and captain my country at international level in particular. In the 1990–91 edition of the *Rothman's Rugby League Yearbook* they looked back and came up with the Great Britain 'Test Team of the 1980s'. It was based on the most appearances in each position. Now, Ellery Hanley played 29 times during the 10 years and so they put him in the centre. Looking at this list here you really do feel proud to be associated with some of the greatest names in British Rugby League:

Mick Burke; Des Drummond, Garry Schofield, Ellery Hanley, Henderson Gill; Tony Myler, Andy Gregory; Kevin Ward, David Watkinson, Lee Crooks, Andy Goodway, Mike Gregory, Harry Pinner.

Amen to that.

12. Bulldogs, Boxers and more

"Our bulldogs have meant just as much to me over the years as anything I have achieved on the rugby field."
Harry Pinner

In the early part of this book I said that my dad had kennels in Merton Bank when I was growing up. I didn't help him as such, but I was always interested in the dogs who were there at the time. My grandad showed wire-haired terriers. He would groom them immaculately before a show and every loose hair was brushed out. I remember him telling me about going to a particular show when one lady walked her dog and she was wearing a short skirt and low-cut blouse. The lady's dog got first prize and my grandad was furious. He went up to the judge and said "You've looked at the wrong end of the lead, there, old lad."

One of the first dogs I had was a boxer called Mandy, who unfortunately was run over when I was just 15. Two years later I drove down to South Wales in a battered old Fiesta and came back with my first bulldog, a female who we called Emma. She produced a few pups and I sold them, but I never thought that I would end up breeding bulldog pups on a much larger scale later on. Obviously the pubs meant that this would have been impossible and it has only been since we left the licensing trade that we have bred pups as a business.

Bulldogs were originally used by farmers to control livestock and, apparently, by the fifteenth century in addition to catching horses, cattle and boars they were also used in a barbaric sport called 'bull-baiting'. Trained dogs would try to get themselves latched on to a tethered bull's nose and not let go until the dog had pulled the bull to the ground, or the bull had killed the dog. So, originally, they were always bred for their aggression and, believe it or not, a dog weighing, say, 80 pounds could bring down a bull weighing almost a ton. They used to corkscrew their body around the bull's neck and toss the bull over its own centre of gravity. So they were not the sort of dogs to be messed with.

These dogs developed a stocky body, with a large head and powerful jaws. When bull-baiting was out-lawed in the *Cruelty to Animals Act* 1835, the bulldog's working days came to an end and they gradually became a favoured pet for many people and are strongly recommended as a pet by me.

I've kept bulldogs for over 30 years and have never been bitten. I love their make-up and temperament; they are so loyal and lovable and safe around children as well. But to breed them requires a lot of time and effort to do what is right for them. At our cottage in Appleton Thorn in Warrington, we had special kennels built for our breeding dogs, with

115

all mod cons. We must have spent a small fortune in getting things right for them. When first born, bulldog pups need 24-hour care, particularly in the first month. We gradually developed a reputation for breeding top quality pups and several of my former team-mates have come to me to buy one, including Peter Glynn.

I love bulldogs and once had to save one of my dogs, Albert, from possibly drowning in the Bridgewater Canal. We had just taken over at the Parr Arms in Grappenhall and I was walking along the bank with my daughter Joanne, who was five at the time. I think the problem was that Joanne was feeding some of the ducks with cheese biscuits and Albert didn't want to be left out.

He jumped into the canal to see if he could pinch a few, but it went badly wrong for him. I think he thought it was just a big puddle. I thought I could just pull him back to the bank, but he was obviously in trouble. He stayed under the water, so I had to dive in and pull him to the surface. It seemed as though he was unconscious, so I got him back on the bank and brought him round. The water was absolutely freezing and I had to walk back to the pub which was about threequarters of a mile away, with my clothes dripping wet. But it was worth it.

I still have the report from the local paper, with the headline: "Dogonne – Rugby star turns hero in canal drama".

Sport of Kings

It is true to say that I was involved in quite a few brawls during my playing career, some not of my own doing, of course and it is fair to say that I am also a big fan of organised boxing. When I was young, aged about 10, I was a member of Lowe House Boxing club in St Helens and took part in a few competitions locally, but nothing too serious. It did trigger a life-long interest in the sport and I have been round the world with my good friend David Stretch – now, sadly, no longer with us – to watch some of Ricky Hatton's fights, including in Las Vegas.

Now, my ultimate boxing hero is Joe Frazier. He was a superb fighter, with a big heart and never took a backward step. And what about that tremendous left hook? Ricky is like a smaller version of Joe. He would take three punches to get that one killer punch in. Fortunately, we knew a guy who worked for Team Hatton, as they called it and we were able to go 'backstage' after a number of his fights. Ricky is a great bloke and we thoroughly enjoyed our nights supporting him.

I have met Joe Frazier at a Sportsman's Dinner – former Warrington Welshman Mike Nicholas had come with me and it was such a golden age for the sport of boxing when there were the likes of Roberto Duran, Sugar Ray Leonard, Marvin Hagler and Thomas 'The Hitman' Hearns. It doesn't quite seem to be the same today.

Man's best friend: Neil Holding is holding my bulldog, Winston, next to the players' tunnel at Knowsley Road. (Photo: Brian Peers)

Our former home at Appleton Thorne was geared to keeping our bulldogs in the best possible conditions. (Photo: Alex Service)

The 'Thrilla in Manilla' was a fantastic fight between Joe Frazier and Mohammed Ali. (Photo: Alex Service)

The chance to meet the great Roberto Duran was too good to miss. (Courtesy Harry Pinner)

Saints' Players' Association functions are always a good opportunity to catch up with former team-mates. This was one of the last at Knowsley Road, in 2009. Left to right: Harry Pinner, Tommy Martyn, Phil Veivers, Mark Bailey, Barry Ledger, Neil Holding, Tommy Frodsham, Alan Hunte, Graham Liptrot, Jon Neill, Paul Loughlin and Denis Litherland (Photo: Alex Service)

Harry's good friend David Stretch (sadly no longer with us) and Harry line up with the formidable Evander Holyfield. Former Warrington star Mike Nicholas is on the right just in case we need him. (Courtesy Harry Pinner)

119

Hook, line and sinker

Fly fishing has also become a passion for me over the years and I seem to have inherited this from my dad, who was a keen fisherman himself. At one time I was mad keen on golf, but I tended to get quite frustrated by it and thought that I might as well take something else up. I had lessons on the River Dee and I've been a keen angler ever since. Graham Bate has been my partner and I began fishing in reservoirs, like the Deva Springs in Hampshire, where I caught a huge 18 pound rainbow trout. The fish itself had pride of place for many years at the Parr Arms, together with my rugby league jerseys. Graham introduced me to fishing the River Wharfe at Boulton Abbey, where it is possible to catch brown trout and grayling. I also fish at Corwen and Llangollen. It may be a rolling river, but the whole experience is one of peace and relaxation, whether we catch anything or not.

Keeping the flame burning

It is always great to meet up with old friends and team-mates, a lot of it courtesy of the Saints' Players' Association, formerly the Past Players, where we can have a natter and remember our playing days. I go to the new stadium at Langtree Park when I can and will always take part in forums and pre-match interviews whenever required. Unfortunately, none of us are getting any younger and several really top class players have passed away in recent years, such as Roger Millward, and it is important that their contribution is recognised by the game as a whole, and the wider world of sport.

I am privileged to have been inducted into the Association's Hall of Fame and to join some very famous names on the list, such as Alf Ellaby, Alex Murphy, Keiron Cunningham and George Nicholls. Also, my career is represented at Langtree Park by one of the many colourful 'splashes' produced by Ken Hughes and his Vinyline company. It really is great to be remembered in this way! When we go round the stadium and look at the lush turf, we really do wish we could turn the clock back.

But regrets in sport? Disappointments, certainly, like not having won at Wembley in 1978 and losing the semi-final 12 months later. Regrets – none. But to captain Great Britain – that was a real dream come true.

13. Home and family

Up in smoke

In May 2010, Anne and I both got the shock of our lives! I honestly thought that the thatched cottage in Appleton Thorn, Warrington, our home for 30 years, was looking spot on for our retirement. Then, one Sunday afternoon I had just settled down to watch some sport in the living room when Anne said that there was a lot smoke coming out of the chimney. I went to check and she was right, but there was a bigger problem. I could see flames all along the ridge and inside flames were also moving across our bedroom roof. That was it – don't panic Captain Mainwaring.

We phoned the fire brigade and in the end, there were five crews on the scene at the height of the blaze. What they had to do was to use scaled ladders to make a fire break in the thatch itself. We were both in shock and managed to get our dogs: four bulldogs and a Highland terrier to safety. Our neighbours also helped us to remove as much furniture as we could and they did a brilliant job. Embers from the living room fire started the blaze in what somebody told me was a million-to-one chance. It was such a shame to see the damage to the house and the firefighters were around until about eight o'clock that night. I don't suppose that they could take any chances with the thatched roof re-igniting. Fortunately we were able to restore the cottage despite the damage and, to be honest, it could have been a whole lot worse and, really, it is a risk for anyone who lives in a thatched property.

My dad passed away in 2010 and opted to have his ashes scattered at sea, relating back to his former life as a merchant seaman. In 2016, my mum was still living in the town they had retired to – Abergele and we visit her regularly. Unfortunately, our family received another huge blow when my 'big' sister, Pat, succumbed to cancer. We were really close and always supported each other as best as we could. I remember Pat wrote several letters to the local press when I was having a bad time or was out of form during my rugby career and this was typical of the support she gave me. I miss her terribly.

Enduring friendships are very important and my mates Jack and Bob have also looked after me well. We manage to have the odd drink or two and enjoy occasional trips to the races. We have even been to Tenerife playing golf. I still get frustrated when I play, but under that blue sky it really doesn't seem to matter that much.

In 2016, Anne and I sold our cottage and moved to a new house in Mobberley in Cheshire, although we are still near to our grandchildren.

Harry's mum Connie and her grand-daughter Joanne enjoy a refreshing drink.
(Courtesy Harry Pinner)

Anne and Harry have been together since the late 1980s.
(Courtesy Harry Pinner)

Harry with his grandchildren. (Courtesy Harry Pinner)

A family affair: Left to right: Sophie (Lee's daughter), Anne, Harry (jr), Harry. Frankie, Joanne, Lee, Lee (jr). (Courtesy Harry Pinner)

We still have a couple of bulldogs, but not on the same scale as we used to. Our daughter, Joanne, went to St Wilfrid's school in Grappenhall and then on to Lymm High School. She was a good swimmer and runner in her day and she married Lee Stewart in 2012. They live in Warrington and Lee was a good sportsman himself, especially at football.

He was on Everton's books and also played for Crewe Alexandra. He is also a Class 1 HGV driver. So far, they have three children: the twins, Lee junior and Harry Anthony, are the oldest, together with Frankie, a really tough young lady, who takes everything that the twins can throw at her. She is also a belting little footballer. Anne and I love the grand kids and we spend as much time with them as we possibly can. They are the future and, you never know, there just might be another fine sportsperson or two to watch and support. After all, like me, it's in their DNA.

Appendix: Statistics and honours

Clubs

St Helens

Season	Apps	Subs	NPS	Tries	Goals	DG	Pts
1975–76	9	0	3	1	0	1	4
1976–77	33	3	0	3	9	2	29
1977–78	44	1	0	20	6	6	78
1978–79	37	0	0	11	18	10	79
1979–80	33	0	0	13	72	9	192
1980–81	28	2	0	6	27	6	78
1981–82	17	2	0	3	4	4	21
1982–83	30	0	0	4	4	13	33
1983–84	34	0	0	4	0	14	30
1984–85	35	1	0	9	0	8	44
1985–86	19	1	0	3	0	0	12
1986–87	3	0	0	1	0	0	4
Totals	**322**	**10**	**3**	**78**	**140**	**73**	**604**

1976–77: Premiership winner
1977–78: Challenge Cup runner-up
1978–79: BBC2 Floodlit Trophy runner-up
1982–83: Lancashire Cup runner-up
1984–85: Lancashire Cup winner & Premiership winner

Widnes

Season	Apps	Subs	NPS	Tries	Goals	DG	Pts
1986–87	23	2	0	2	0	0	8
1987–88	12	1	0	0	0	1	1
Totals	**35**	**3**	**0**	**2**	**0**	**1**	**9**

Leigh

Season	Apps	Subs	NPS	Tries	Goals	DG	Pts
1987–88	11	0	0	0	0	0	0

Bradford Northern

Season	Apps	Subs	NPS	Tries	Goals	DG	Pts
1988–89	20	4	0	1	0	0	4

Carlisle

Season	Apps	Subs	NPS	Tries	Goals	DG	Pts
1989–90	11	0	0	1	0	0	4

Representative matches

Lancashire (County Championship)
Saints' Lancashire Heritage Number: 68

Date	Teams	Venue	Position	Pts
02/02/77	Lancashire 18 Cumbria 14	Leigh	NPS	0
01/03/77	Yorkshire 18 Lancashire 13	Castleford	Sub (for D. Boyd)	0
27/09/78	Lancashire 23 Yorkshire 7	Widnes	Sub (for G. Nicholls)	0
11/10/78	Cumbria 16 Lancashire 15	Whitehaven	Sub (for E. Prescott)	0
05/09/79	Lancashire 23 Cumbria 15	St Helens	Loose forward	DG
12/09/79	Yorkshire 19 Lancashire 16	Castleford	Loose forward	2T DG
09/09/81	Yorkshire 21 Lancashire 15	Castleford	Loose forward	0
16/09/81	Lancashire 15 Cumbria 27	Wigan	Loose forward	0

Overall: Appearances: 4+3 NP Sub (1) Won: 3 Lost: 5 Tries: 2 DG: 2 Points: 8

Great Britain Under-24s

Date	Teams	Venue	Position	Pts
14/11/76	Great Britain 19 France 2	Hull	Loose forward	0
05/12/76	France 9 Great Britain 11	Albi	Loose forward	DG
12/11/77	Great Britain 27 France 9	Hull	Sub (for T. Skerrett)	0
18/12/77	France 4 Great Britain 8	Tonneins	Sub (for M. Gibbins)	0
04/10/78	Great Britain 8 Australia 30	Hull KR	Sub (for P. Smith)	0
14/01/79	France 3 Great Britain 15	Limoux	Sub (for B. Case)	0
24/11/79	Great Britain 14 France 2	Leigh	Loose forward	0
13/01/80	France 7 Great Britain 11	Carcassonne	Loose forward	0

Overall: Appearances: 4+4 Won: 7 Lost: 1 DG: 1 Points: 1

126

England (European Championship)

England Heritage Number: 520

Date	Teams	Venue	Position	Pts
29/02/1980	England 26 Wales 9	Hull KR	Loose forward	2DG
16/03/1980	France 2 England 4	Narbonne	Loose forward	0
21/02/1981	England 1 France 5	Leeds	Loose forward	0

Overall: Appearances: 3 Won: 2 Lost: 1 DG: 2 Points: 2

Great Britain (Test matches)

Selected for the 1984 Great Britain Lions squad for the 1984 tour to Australia and New Zealand.

Date	TM	Teams	Venue	Position	Pts
18/10/80	TM 211	GB 14 New Zealand 14	Wigan	Sub (for T. Skerrett)	0
02/11/80	TM 212	GB 8 New Zealand 12	Odsal	Loose forward	0
19/10/85	TM 232	GB 22 New Zealand 24	Leeds	Loose forward (Capt)	0
02/11/85	TM 233	GB 25 New Zealand 8	Wigan	Loose forward (Capt)	DG
09/11/85	TM 234	GB 6 New Zealand 6	Leeds	Loose forward (Capt)	0
16/02/86	TM 235	France 10 GB 10	Avignon	Loose forward (Capt)	0
22/11/86	TM 239	GB 15 Australia 24	Wigan	Loose forward	0

TM: Official test match number

Overall: Appearances: 7 +1 Won: 1 Drawn: 3 Lost: 3 DG: 1 Points: 1

1984 tour appearances for Great Britain (non test matches):
18 May: Northern Territory
27 May: Western Division
2 June: Newcastle (Sub)
11 June: Wide Bay
17 June: North Queensland
20 June: Toowoomba
28 June: Northern Rivers

All first-class matches

Apps	Sub	NPS	Tries	Goals	DG	Pts
423	26	4	84	140	79	632

Individual Honours

Young Player of the Year Nominee:
1976–77 (awarded to David Ward)

First Division Player of the Year Nominee:
1977–78 (awarded to George Nicholls)
1984–85 (awarded to Ellery Hanley)

Harry Sunderland Trophy winner 1985

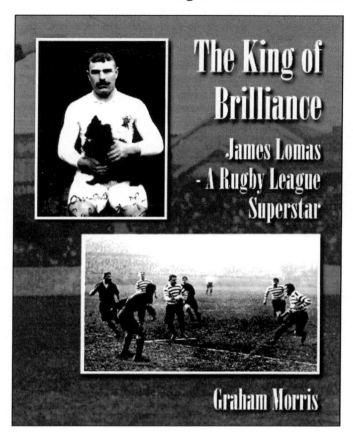

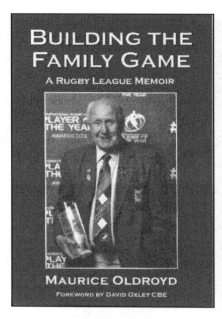

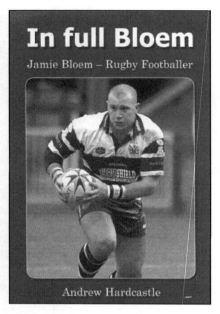

Maurice Oldroyd was one of the key people involved in the development of amateur rugby league since the foundation of the British Amateur Rugby League Association (BARLA) in 1973.

He was the Association's first full-time employee, and played a major role in its development until his retirement in 2000. However, he then became the Association's chairman from 2001 to 2005, and today is the Association's patron. This fascinating memoir reflects on his life and involvement in rugby league. Maurice Oldroyd has been at the centre of amateur rugby league since 1973. This well- illustrated, fascinating memoir is essential reading for all rugby league fans. Published at £12.95, available for **just £5.00 post free in the UK** from www.llpshop.co.uk or by post from London League Publications Ltd, PO Box 65784, London NW2 9NS.

In full Bloem: The explosive biography of South African rugby league star Jamie Bloem, current referee and former Castleford, Oldham, Halifax, Widnes, Doncaster and Huddersfield player. He also played regularly for South Africa, and was capped by Scotland.

Published in February 2013 @ £14.95 (hardback), just £8.95 post free in the UK direct from London League Publications Ltd.

All our books can be ordered from any bookshop @ full price. To order direct from London League Publications Ltd visit our website: www.llpshop.co.uk or write to LLP, PO Box 65784, London NW2 9NS (cheques payable to London League Publications Ltd). Most of our books are available as E-Books for Kindle from Amazon.

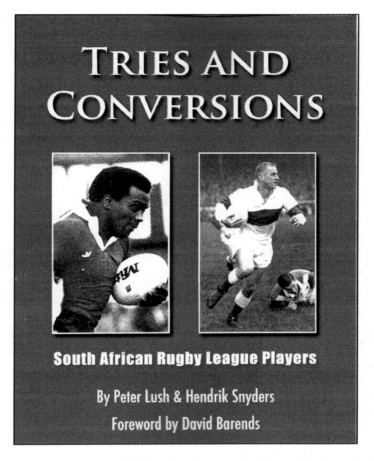

TRIES AND CONVERSIONS

South African Rugby League Players

By Peter Lush & Hendrik Snyders

Foreword by David Barends

In 1910, James Megson and William Mart became the first native-born South Africans to sign for British rugby league clubs. Since then, South African players have made a significant contribution to rugby league. This book is the first comprehensive study of their contribution to rugby league. It covers players who played in Great Britain and Australia. Some were very successful, such as Attie van Heerden and George van Rooyen in the 1920s, Tom van Vollenhoven, Alan Skene, Jan Prinsloo and Len Killeen in the 1950s and 1960s, and Mark Johnson and Jamie Bloem in the Super League era. But there were also players who never made it after switching codes to play rugby league, and their stories are also told here.

Available for just £13.95 post free in the UK direct from London League Publications Ltd or from Amazon.co.uk . Credit card orders via www.llpshop.co.uk; payment by cheque to PO Box 65784, London NW2 9NS. Available in bookshops at £14.95.
Also available as an E-Book for Kindle from Amazon.

The Glory and the Dream is a great new rugby league novel. It tells the story of a young boy's rite of passage. It is full of rich characters, and is played out against a backdrop of social upheaval in the austere post-war years of rationing and shortages. But it was a time when communities pulled together. Walking days, royal visits, Sunday School outings to the seaside and communal bonfire nights were annual highlights. It was a time when youngsters had to make their own entertainment, including playing rugby league. It is about Johnny Gregson, the young star of the

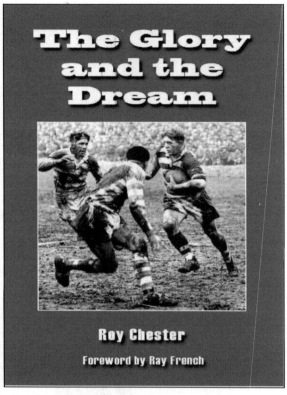

Garton rugby league team, whose dream is to follow his dad's success in the sport. Johnny lives with his mother in Four Locks, a poor working class area in a grimy northern town. His father died in the Second World War. The story starts in 1945, when Johnny is aged 10. It follows his rise from junior rugby league through playing rugby union as a schoolboy to turning professional with Garton.

Johnny faces challenges at every turn, including when he wins a scholarship to a local public school and is labelled as a 'slum kid;' by the class bully. His prowess at rugby helps him deal with this boy. Also, at the tender age of 16, he meets a young woman who becomes very important to him. This is a story about sport, romance and working class life. It includes many humorous incidents, insights and even tragedy in a young man's development.

Published in March 2014 at £9.95. Order for just £5.00 post free in the UK from www.llpshop.co.uk from London League Publications Ltd, PO Box 65784, London NW2 9NS

Also available as an E-Book for Kindle from Amazon.

Soldiers' League
The story of Army Rugby League
By Sean Fanning

"Rugby league epitomises all of the qualities required of a soldier – skill, fitness, courage, teamwork, determination and a strong sense of discipline."
Lieutenant General Sir Scott Grant, former President Army Rugby League.

Rugby league only became a recognised sport in the Army in 1994. However, since then it has thrived, overcoming many obstacles on the way. This book is the first to be published about rugby league in the Armed Forces. It covers the growth and development of the sport in the Army.

Sean Fanning, born and raised in St Helens, played professional rugby league for Leigh and Highfield. He was a Staff Sergeant in the Army Medical Service until 2014, and was on active duty in Afghanistan in 2012. He has played for and coached the Army Rugby League team, played for the Great Britain Armed Forces team in the 2008 Armed Forces World Cup and has played for Combined Services. Sean's share of the profits from this book will go to Soldiers' League, which raises money for service

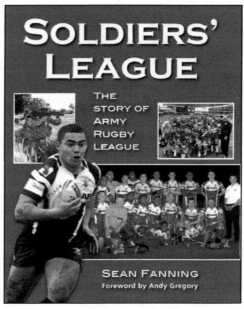

charities, including the Royal British Legion, Blesma and Combat Stress.

Published in 2013 @ £14.95, now available direct from London League Publications Ltd at www.llpshop.co.uk for just £14.00 (£10 for current or former members of the Armed Forces) post free in the UK or by post from London League Publications Ltd, PO Box 65784, London NW2 9NS.

Also available as an E-Book for Kindle from Amazon.

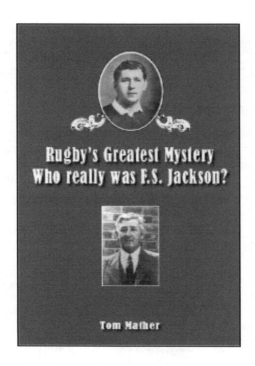

A true life rugby detective story

This is the story of a man whose life was made up of mystery, intrigue and deception, but was also a Rugby Union star before the First World War. He played for Leicester and Cornwall when they won the 1908 County Championship. He was selected for the Anglo-Welsh Rugby Union tour to New Zealand and Australia in 1908. However, the RFU recalled him from the tour and banned him from the sport over allegations that he was a professional player, and had played for Swinton in the Northern Union. The scandal around his suspension from rugby union caused great problems for the RFU and almost saw a further split in the game.

He then played rugby league for New Zealand, against the British Lions in 1910. After the First World War he was reinstated by the New Zealand RU, became an East Coast selector and saw his son play for the All Blacks. For around 60 years he used the name Frederick Stanley Jackson, even though it was not his given name. When he died in 1957 he took to the grave his true identity. Even his family knew little about his early years in England, or even where he came from. **It was a mystery that remained unresolved until now.** The book also includes an analysis of the development of Leicester Tigers RFC up to the First World War.

Published in March 2012 at £12.95. Special offer £6.95 post free in the UK available direct from London League Publications Ltd, PO Box 65784, London NW2 9NS (cheques payable to London League Publications Ltd)
credit card orders via our website: www.llpshop.co.uk or order from any bookshop. Also available as an E-Book for Kindle from Amazon.

Braver than all the rest
A mother fights for her son

Philip Howard

Dave and Sarah Burgess are devastated when their young son Karl is found to have muscular dystrophy. Then another tragedy hits the family hard. But the family are committed to do the best they can for Karl, who has a passion for rugby league. Based in Castleton, a Yorkshire town near the border with Lancashire, Karl's determination to get the most out of life, despite his disability, inspires those around him, in particular Chris Anderton, one of the Castleton Rugby League Club players, who is coming to the end of his career in the game. A moving novel of family life and rugby league. **Author Philip Howard is originally from St Helens.**

Published in 2010 at £9.95, special offer £7.00 post free in UK direct from London League Publications Ltd. Credit card orders via www.llpshop.co.uk orders by cheque to LLP, PO Box 65784, London NW2 9NS

Also available as an E-Book on Kindle for Amazon.

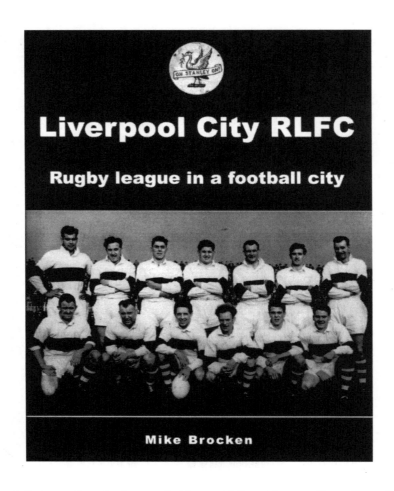

Liverpool City RLFC

Rugby league in a football city

Mike Brocken

The full story of rugby league in Liverpool from the sport's earliest days to the modern era.
Based on extensive research and interviews, a fascinating story of a struggle against the odds.

246 page paperback available direct from London League Publications Ltd for £14.95 post free in the UK. Visit www.llpshop.co.uk to order (credit cards via Pay Pal) or write to London League Publications Ltd, PO Box 65784 London NW2 9NS (cheques payable to London League Publications Ltd).

Also available as an E-Book for Kindle on Amazon.